Teaching Interpersonal Communication:
A Guidebook

Teaching Interpersonal Communication: A Guidebook

SECOND EDITION

ALICIA ALEXANDER
SOUTHERN ILLINOIS UNIVERSITY EDWARDSVILLE

ELIZABETH J. NATALLE
UNIVERSITY OF NORTH CAROLINA, GREENSBORO

BEDFORD / ST. MARTIN'S
Boston ◆ New York

For Bedford/St. Martin's

Vice President, Editorial, Macmillan Higher Education Humanities: Edwin Hill
Publisher for Communication: Erika Gutierrez
Editorial Assistants: Joanna Kamouh, Catherine Burgess
Publishing Services Coordinator: Lidia MacDonald-Carr
Senior Production Supervisor: Lisa McDowell
Marketing Manager: Tom Digiano
Project Management: Books By Design, Inc.
Copy Editor: Books By Design, Inc.
Director of Rights and Permissions: Hilary Newman
Senior Art Director: Anna Palchik
Cover Design: Billy Boardman
Composition: Achorn International, Inc.
Printing and Binding: RR Donnelley.

Manufactured in the United States of America.

9   8   7   6   5   4
f   e   d   c   b   a

For information, write: Bedford/St. Martin's, 75 Arlington Street, Boston, MA 02116
  (617-399-4000)

ISBN 978-1-4576-8109-7

Preface

What students learn in the interpersonal communication course never stays just in the classroom. Studies show that the people who succeed in business, marriage, and other domains in life are those who can effectively communicate with others. This is why our course is so important, and why we've got to be sure we're teaching it right. No matter their major, students need basic training in interpersonal communication, and now that they are utilizing more computer-mediated forms of communication they need a broader sense of communication skills. Thus, it's time for us as interpersonal communication professors to look again at our curriculum and make sure students leave the classroom equipped with the skills they need to competently communicate in a constantly evolving landscape. This leads us to consider: What are our roles as teachers of interpersonal communication? How can we help our students improve their basic communication skills in order to ensure that they engage in more productive, healthy, and worthwhile relationships? Using the combined advice and experiences of myself and Professor Elizabeth Natalle, *Teaching Interpersonal Communication* answers those questions and provides information and references to make teaching easier.

When I was asked to write for the second edition of *Teaching Interpersonal Communication*, I was honored and excited to take on the challenge. The first edition, written solely by Elizabeth, intended to help instructors develop more effective interpersonal communication courses, and that intention was greatly fulfilled. I used the first edition in my own graduate course, Seminar in Communication Education, to help prepare my students for their first year as teaching assistants and future faculty. My students profoundly appreciated the specific advice, teaching strategies, support, and inspiration Elizabeth offered. While rewriting the second edition, I aimed to add my own experience to provide a new perspective and fresh advice to help new and seasoned instructors as they develop their interpersonal communication courses.

Over the years, I've noticed that too many new instructors get "handed off" to teach the entry-level interpersonal communication course as if it were a simple class to teach. Those of us who are more experienced in the field and in the classroom know that teaching the course is far from easy. Further taxing the new instructor is the fact that she or he may have taken fewer interpersonal courses than those of us who have "grown up" with the discipline. New instructors need an opportunity to develop a strong sense of the theory and discipline necessary to teach an interpersonal course with integrity, and they need guidance and support to overcome the problems and barriers to teaching the class effectively.

Teaching Interpersonal Communication: A Guidebook, Second Edition, serves as a guide and reference book for new instructors, adjuncts, and others with less experience teaching interpersonal communication courses. You will find advice on constructing a syllabus, managing a classroom, selecting instructional strategies, constructing exams, and developing as a professional teacher for traditional, hybrid, and online class formats. This book is about *teaching*, and it is designed to demonstrate how to integrate pedagogy and content to create a more effective course. It also provides avenues for developing and strengthening one's theoretical context. In this regard, even experienced teachers from all types of teaching institutions may benefit from this book.

The second edition of *Teaching Interpersonal Communication* is divided into two sections: Part I, "Teaching Notes," consists of five chapters that mentor instructors in both personal development and course logistics. Chapter 1, "Teaching Approach and Philosophy," begins the mentoring process by asking the reader to consider himself or herself as a teacher in general and to set goals for becoming a better teacher. Chapter 2, "The Basic Tool of Effective Teaching: The Syllabus," is devoted to the syllabus as the basic tool of effective teaching. Chapter 3, "Student Challenges and Problematics," discusses common classroom issues, including using space, managing discussion, and setting up course policies and rules. It also discusses student challenges like disruptive students, nontraditionals, and co-cultural students. Chapter 4, "Instructional Strategies," examines five structural issues that affect the technical decisions an instructor makes to deliver an effective course: instructional strategies; balancing theory and practice; vocabulary; use of technology; and service learning. Chapter 5, "Evaluation and Assessment," studies logistical concerns such as constructing assignments to support learning objectives, developing a grading system, and participating in assessment procedures. By the close of Part I, we will have taken a comprehensive look at a system for teaching interpersonal communication.

Part II, "Teaching Resources," consists of two chapters that show readers how teaching can be informed from the discipline's theory and literature. Chapter 6, "Teaching Online Courses in Interpersonal Communication," is a completely new chapter for this edition that highlights the benefits of teaching interpersonal communication in online formats; the differences between online interpersonal courses and face-to-face courses; strategies for engaging online learners; suggestions for course development, organization, and grading; and the challenges of teaching interpersonal communication online and in hybrid formats. Chapter 7, "Foundational Resources," offers a list of primary sources we judge important for one's professional development as a teacher of interpersonal communication. This chapter also provides an annotated bibliography of eighty-five classic and new sources that support a basic course.

Teaching Interpersonal Communication spearheaded Bedford/St. Martin's Professional Resource Series for Communication. This series was conceived specifically for instructors seeking best practices for instructing, managing, and developing a course. When asked to write this text, we accepted not only because we are passionate about the topic, but also because we are impressed with the editorial team's belief that a textbook publishing firm should attend to the needs of both students *and* professors. Thus, *Teaching Interpersonal Communication*, Second Edition, not only offers sound advice and practical tips for good teaching; more specifically, it also approaches the introductory interpersonal course with a balanced integration of theory and practice.

It has been my pleasure to work with all those involved in the writing, editing, and production of this book: Denise Wydra, Erika Gutierrez, Noel Hohnstine, Joanna Kamouh, marketing manager Tom Digiano, and assistant production editor Lidia MacDonald-Carr. In particular, I wish to thank Noel Hohnstine for careful editing of the manuscript and guidance as we worked to make the second edition more intuitive for instructors.

This book would not exist without Elizabeth Natalle and her influences, including her colleagues around the country and at the University of North Carolina at Greensboro: Jen Baker, Marion Boyer, Michelle Burch, Lynn Weber Cannon, David Carlone, Elise Dallimore, Jessica Delk, Steve McCornack, Kelly Morrison, Mark Orbe, Robyn Parker, Chris Poulos, Bill Rawlins, Jen Day Shaw, and Julia Wood. I would also like to express my appreciation to my colleagues in the Department of Applied Communication Studies at Southern Illinois University Edwardsville (SIUE) and elsewhere for sharing their wisdom throughout the chapters. I am especially thankful to Jocelyn DeGroot for helping me in writing the chapter on "Teaching Online Courses in Interpersonal Communication." I have learned so much from her about computer-mediated communication and teaching online courses, and I am thankful for her friendship.

I would like to thank all of my undergraduate students in my interpersonal communication courses as well as my teaching assistants over the last eleven years at SIUE. Finally, I would like to thank the three professors who most influenced my career during my years in my doctoral program at the University of Texas at Austin: Dr. Mark Knapp, Dr. John Daly, and my dissertation adviser, Dr. Anita Vangelisti. Your passion for the field and your students is inspirational.

I wish to dedicate this book to my husband, Craig, and my three children, Jack, Gemma, and Maya, for always supporting my career and understanding my passion for interpersonal communication.

Alicia Alexander

Contents

Teaching Interpersonal Communication:
A Guidebook

Teaching Notes

CHAPTER

1

Teaching Approach and Philosophy

Teaching is an honor and earns the respect of others. As teachers of interpersonal communication, we bring honor both to the communication discipline and to the process that binds people together in society. Educating others is a serious responsibility that requires a teacher to know him- or herself before the imparting, negotiating, and interpreting of knowledge in the classroom can ever begin. How well do you know yourself as a teacher? As a person? Perhaps philosopher Martin Buber (1970) is correct that we are always *becoming* and never quite at a stage of *being*. Or, perhaps, as anthropologist Mary Catherine Bateson (1989) said, we compose our lives as improvisations in an ever-changing world. Life does not allow us to rest or become static. As professional educators, then, our goal is to become the best teachers we can be. Naturally, becoming our best will continue over the entire course of our careers.

We begin this book with an assumption: Although we are the "authors" and you are the "reader," know that we are unified as college and university teachers who strive to be our best. Indeed, we hope this book will serve as a guide for teaching interpersonal communication. In this chapter we invite you to think about your approach to teaching. Based on your history and professional training, what would you identify as your strengths and weaknesses? What is your overall teaching philosophy? What are some of your professional goals?

CONSIDERING YOURSELF AS A TEACHER

You are a teacher, and you have what educator Parker Palmer describes as "the courage to teach" (Intrator, 2002). That's a good starting point, but have you ever thought about your history as a teacher? When did you know you wanted to become an educator? How has that knowledge shaped you to date? For us, we both have wanted to be teachers since we were in elementary school. We made decisions throughout our education that were relevant to our training as teachers. Elizabeth majored in education as an undergraduate at the University of Central Florida, volunteered in public schools, and taught courses for no fee as a graduate student in order to further her knowledge and experience. Alicia was coaching her friends and family about interpersonal communication since she took her first class in interpersonal communication theory at Missouri State University her sophomore year. We call ourselves *teacher* or *professor* when describing who we are to others because it is the single most important aspect of our professional identities. What types of experiences have you had that likely prepared you for a career in teaching? If, for example, you have volunteered for Big Brothers Big Sisters or were a Girl Scout or a Boy Scout, then you have gained experience that will help you teach. How have your experiences affected your basic ability to stand up in front of a group of learners and teach interpersonal communication as a college course? Beyond technical preparation in public speaking and organizing groups of people, how have those experiences shaped your basic approach to teaching?

In *The Joy of Teaching* (2005), Peter Filene, an awarding-winning teacher at the University of North Carolina at Chapel Hill, says that teaching is collaborative and personal. He likes to think about the student-teacher relationship as "heightened conversation." In other words, Filene sees teaching as an interpersonal relationship. He uses the strength of this interpersonal teaching style to focus on the learning relationship and be a "joyful," or successful, teacher. Professor Filene challenges his readers right away to consider themselves as teachers and ask, "Who am I?" We can't think of a better question. Once you consider your history and training, you will be able to identify your current strengths and challenges. Having a baseline allows you to teach with self-knowledge. Knowing that you will continue to evolve as both a person and a teacher, you can look forward to your own future with confidence. Think about some of your strengths and challenges as a teacher and record them below.

My strengths as a teacher

_____

_____

_____

_____

_____

My challenges as a teacher

_____

_____

_____

_____

_____

Until now, we have been reflecting on you as a teacher to try to frame your background and training. What we hope you have concluded at this point is that, although you undoubtedly have much to offer, you may still benefit from some additional professional development. We now turn to a more elusive topic — an ongoing goal you should try to achieve throughout your career: effective teaching.

EFFECTIVE TEACHING

What is effective teaching? Are all teachers effective? How can a teacher become more effective? Am *I* effective as a teacher? We have been thinking about these questions since our first experiences teaching in the university classroom (over thirty years ago for Elizabeth and almost twenty years ago for Alicia), and we are still working toward being the most effective teachers possible. These are not rhetorical questions, nor are they especially easy to answer. From a social science perspective, we have been testing teacher behavior for many years to pinpoint variables that contribute to teaching effectiveness (Frymier & Houser, 2000; Nussbaum, 1992); we will discuss some of that research in Chapter 3. In the section that follows we will explore the practical steps one can take on the journey toward professional success and discuss how a solid teaching philosophy can serve as the central component, or foundation, of any course. We will also look at how we can continuously improve our teaching by taking advantage of professional development opportunities. These pragmatic goals serve as the theme for this book: to provide an organic look at what it takes to teach an effective class in interpersonal communication at the entry level.

Start-up Difficulties in Effective Teaching

There are a couple of ironies about effective teaching that we must face up front: first, although interpersonal communication is considered a core course in the field (Wardrope, 1999), we do not have enough qualified teachers to handle the demands of the class. It takes a highly experienced teacher to integrate his or her life experience with the theoretical knowledge delivered in the classroom. As with public speaking, there is often a need for interpersonal teachers, and we expect new MAs to pay their dues by starting their teaching careers with these two courses.

A similar situation occurs when temporary instructors or graduate students are given the responsibility of teaching the interpersonal communication course just because one more section of the course needs to be offered. For some inexplicable reason, there is a myth in our field that anyone can teach the interpersonal communication course. The faulty reasoning behind this myth is that we all participate in interpersonal relationships and, therefore, we all should be able to teach interpersonal communication. Wrong! There is a significant difference between *being in relationships* and *knowing how to teach the interpersonal communication process*. This myth infiltrated Elizabeth's department, as you can see in the following constructive feedback given by a graduating senior in her capstone portfolio narrative:

> There should be more consistency in the department. . . . I enrolled in relational communication three semesters before finally staying in the class. The second time I enrolled in the class I thought the class was more of a joke. . . . One girl asked, "My boyfriend will not talk to me, what do I do?" The class members put their two cents worth in and we related nothing to the book or anything else relevant. I then dropped the class . . . it felt like a three day a week counseling session instead of a class. (Burke, 2005)

This type of feedback is not uncommon, and it testifies to the fact that we need to mentor instructors in these situations to grow and develop the skills appropriate to teaching the course. The question then becomes: What is effective teaching and what is it within the context of teaching interpersonal communication? What do you do as a new instructor who is under contract to teach this course as a new preparation? We recommend that you situate your technical skills (e.g., knowing how to create a syllabus, guiding discussions, grading assignments, and so on) within a larger teaching philosophy.

Coming to Effective Teaching through a Teaching Philosophy

To be a competent teacher, one needs both technical expertise (knowledge of the subject matter; teaching skills) and a philosophy of teaching. Your own education provides you with the basic knowledge of interpersonal theory and concepts (see Graham & Shue, 2001, for a template on how to organize that knowledge); your life experience provides the working laboratory for application of knowledge; and time allows you to synthesize and evaluate knowledge and experience so that it becomes coherent and meaningful. Knowledge of pedagogy may or may not be a part of your educational training, and this book can help you with that. Although you can learn the technical expertise over a period of time, developing a philosophy of teaching to ensure effectiveness in teaching is, in our view, much more difficult to craft and apply.

A philosophy of teaching comprises a system of principles or a holistic viewpoint of how to impart your knowledge of interpersonal communication to students. This philosophy is grounded in cultural values, ethics, and morals. Developing a philosophy toward teaching interpersonal communication is somewhat difficult because cultural prescriptions for communicating, actual life experience, and the ideal prescriptions in textbooks may not always agree with one another. Because everyone has participated in relationships before entering the classroom, we all (teachers and students) come to the classroom with a mindset already in place that helps us approach relationships with a framework for seeing, doing, valuing, and responding in the social world. This comes from actual life experience as dyadic partners.

In the classroom, an interpersonal relationship develops between teacher and student. Again, learning relationships are deeply embedded in cultural conceptions of both how learning should manifest and what the relationship between student and teacher should be. Onto these two layers we add the content of the interpersonal communication course, which is a kind of metacommunication, or commentary, on the previous two layers. This is somewhat frightening to think about because, at any time, negative experiences from real-life relationships could jeopardize the content and/or the relationships involved in the teaching-learning process. But instead of dwelling on the negative possibilities, let's acknowledge that an interpersonal communication class is complicated because of the intersection of theory and real life. Developing a teaching philosophy toward communication is something that takes time and requires a balance in one's thinking about the ideal possibilities versus the messiness of the real world.

In trying to express a teaching philosophy, we like to think of cartography, or mindmapping. One of Elizabeth's greatest inspirations comes from novelist Cormac McCarthy. In *Cities of the Plain* (1998), the protagonist, Billy Parham, meets a fellow traveler on the road. In a long, lyrical discussion on life, the latter says:

> For now I can only say that I had hoped for a sort of calculus that would sum the convergence of map and life when life was done. For within their limitations there must be a common shape or shared domain between the telling and the told. And if that is so then the picture also in whatever partial form must have a direction to it and if it does then whatever is to come must lie in that path. (pp. 273-274)

Elizabeth thinks about this passage a great deal because she is an advocate of mindmaps. She believes that each individual's cognitive mindset and life experience converge and carry that person forward on a path. *Philosophy, mindmap, calculus* — it doesn't matter what vocabulary you use, as long as there is a framework to guide you in your action as a teacher. You help shape students as they develop maps of interpersonal communication to guide themselves on the path of life. What tools help in this shaping process? New teachers are often influenced by their mentors, by their peers, and by university workshops, as well as by the course textbook, which can be a source of both philosophy and knowledge. For example, examine a text such as John Stewart's *Bridges Not Walls* (2002) and you see a humanistic philosophy in the tradition of Martin Buber, Carl Rogers, and Jack Gibb; meanwhile, a text such as Steven McCornack's *Reflect and Relate* (2013) uses a social science approach that covers a broad range of research findings to help the learner approach a dyad with basic communication competence. Neither of these approaches alone is perfect, and a new teacher may not even be aware that the text itself is guiding his or her thinking and philosophical approach. A seasoned teacher, on the other hand, may supplement the text to fit his or her philosophy. Julia Wood and Lisa Lenze (1991) had to compensate for interpersonal communication texts that did not reflect their feminist philosophy to teach with gender inclusivity. Many texts are now more in tune with our times, but the point is that unless you have a teaching philosophy, you do not have a complete approach to teaching. The text is only a starting point, so choose wisely and adjust as your philosophy develops over time.

Let's examine a statement of teaching philosophy made by David Worley, the recipient of the 2001 Central States Communication Association (CSCA) Outstanding New Teacher Award. In Worley's CSCA address, reprinted in *Communication Studies* (Worley, 2001), he demonstrates all that we have talked about here: He integrates his understanding of the nature of teaching (a lifelong impulse) with an orientation on teaching (student-centered) and places communication at the center of the process ("teaching *is* communication"). His basic principles include three ideas: that teaching is a humanistic endeavor in which students and teachers come together authentically; that course material should be relevant to students; and that teachers should engage students in active learning in the classroom.

A slightly different statement, one based more on the framework of the classical philosophers Aristotle and Cicero, is evident in Paaige Turner's (2001) address. Professor Turner, the other CSCA teaching award winner for 2001, also supports the concept of an interactive classroom in which everyone is a teacher and a learner. Although her statement is more technical, relating structural (e.g., lesson plans) and operational (e.g., class activities, exams) procedures for effective teaching, it is a good example of how to think through the manifestation of philosophy in your actual teaching. Reading Worley's and Turner's statements can provide inspiration for your own teaching philosophy. Put your working statement in the teaching portfolio we will discuss later in this chapter, and try to rework it at least once a year.

Now let's turn to effective teaching across a range of disciplines to see what good teachers *think* as they approach the process of teaching.

What Effective Teachers Think

Ken Bain, Director of the Center for Teaching Excellence at New York University, came to the University of North Carolina at Greensboro and spoke to the faculty from his book *What the Best College Teachers Do* (2004). Arriving at the lecture hall, along with about 150 other faculty members, Elizabeth noted and was impressed by the other audience members. There were a number of teaching excellence award winners, many new assistant professors — some with whom she had engaged in lengthy discussions about pedagogy — and a group of professors whose names she had heard mentioned repeatedly by the students as "good" teachers. Over the next hour, Bain shared findings from his fifteen-year study with great teachers. As you might guess, the study found that the technical expertise demonstrated by effective teachers is learned, and that such teachers have a formidable working knowledge of their disciplines. These teachers learned classroom techniques along the way. But something bigger is at stake: Bain's study demonstrates that effective teachers approach teaching with a philosophy about human learning. After all the practices Bain (2004) describes in each chapter (preparation, expectations, conducting class, evaluation techniques), he boils it down to this eloquent statement:

> The magic does not, however, lie in any one of these practices. I cannot stress enough the simple yet powerful notion that the key to understanding the best teaching can be found not in particular practices or rules but in the *attitudes* of the teachers, in their *faith* in their students' abilities to achieve, in their *willingness* to take their students seriously and to let them assume control of their own education, and in their *commitment* to let all policies and practices flow from central learning objectives and from a mutual respect and agreement between students and teachers. (pp. 78–79)

Look at the four philosophical precepts that frame Bain's findings: attitudes, faith, willingness, and commitment. These are powerful concepts to consider as you think through your own philosophy, and we recommend Bain's book as part of that process.

In our field, Bill Rawlins of Ohio University is an exemplar of Bain's idea that good teachers have a philosophy of human learning. In his essay "Teaching as a Mode of Friendship," Rawlins (2000) demonstrates that his research interests in dialectics and friendship converge with his teaching of interpersonal communication to form a mature teaching philosophy. The notion that we can learn together with all members of the class bringing knowledge to bear on life experience is inherent to Rawlins's philosophy. He sees teaching as the Aristotelian notion of friendship that embodies affection, equality, and mutuality so that classroom communication manifests goodwill as learners examine and create knowledge about relationships. Notice that Rawlins easily captures Bain's characteristics of attitudes, faith, willingness, and commitment. Once you read Rawlins's essay, you will fully appreciate his commitment to the teacher-student relationship.

However, the very idea that teaching is a mode of friendship is fraught with tension. Rawlins (2000) skillfully examines how common tensions in friendships manifest in the classroom. Through both his research (Rawlins, 1992) and his teaching experience, Rawlins observed that the four tensions of educational friendship comprise "the dialectics of the freedom to be independent and the freedom to be dependent, affection and instrumentality, judgment and acceptance, and expressiveness and protectiveness" (Rawlins, 2000, p. 8). Rawlins clarified his four tensions based on citations from passages written by his former students about those tensions. What fascinates me is the issue raised around *friendship* versus *being friendly*. Although Rawlins is personally committed to friendship, the student passages reveal a greater admiration and appreciation for a *friendly* classroom, where developing a friendship was more of a potential than an actuality. Rawlins certainly recognizes the problem inherent in negotiating what is comfortable for students and teachers, and he engages the reader in an excellent discussion of both the virtues and the limitations of educational friendship. What I like so much about this essay is the deep level of commitment to a philosophy that requires hard work and a payoff for all involved when the process works. Rawlins concludes:

> It [teaching as a mode of friendship] involves conscientious and disciplined practices, persistent orientations and sensitivities, and lived convictions. The rewards of these activities are their ongoing accomplishment, enriched relationships with fellow learners, and, it is hoped, enhanced humanity and education. (Rawlins, 2000, p. 25)

In the realm of interpersonal communication, what could be more fundamental than enhanced humanity and education?

Mark Orbe, a winner of six teaching and mentoring awards at Western Michigan University, is known for his core concept of *dumela*. Elizabeth asked Professor Orbe to explain this after he visited her campus and she saw this concept in action. Read his response in the following box and then think about your own core concepts as a possible starting point for crafting a statement of teaching philosophy.

FROM THE CLASSROOM: Affirmation and Community as Teaching Philosophy

Dumela is a greeting used by the Basotho (Basutu) people, who live primarily in the northern parts of South Africa; it is Sesotho (Asutu) dialect. I was first introduced to the greeting by my pastor, who began to use it after a trip to South Africa. *Dumela* translates into "good day," but also connotatively communicates "I affirm you, I believe in you, and I see the great potential in you." I've been teaching the basic interpersonal communication class since 1991, and try to incorporate different things each time I teach the course. In 1994 I decided to start each class period by using "Dumela!"

Conceptually, the use of *dumela* fits perfectly with my teaching style. For many students, college is both an exciting and a daunting endeavor. By using this greeting affirmation, I communicate several important messages to my students—hopefully messages that are repeated/enhanced through other forms of communication. In many ways, it helps set the tone of the course—in which all individuals will be respected and affirmed as part of a diverse learning community. We may have contrasting ideas about different interpersonal topics (racism, sexism, language, sexual harassment, etc.), but when we become engaged with these subject matters true dialogue is possible because we begin with a sense of mutual respect, desire for understanding, and genuine affirmation. All this involves affirming where people come from, where they currently exist, as well as where their current learning will take them. In this regard, using the greeting *dumela* facilitates community in- and outside of the classroom.

Mark P. Orbe

Western Michigan University

SOURCE: Personal correspondence with Elizabeth Natalle, May 3, 2006.

DEVELOPING A TEACHING PHILOSOPHY

To help you get started on your teaching philosophy, we'd like to share some information on our own statements as well as some resources that will further assist you. First, know that it is natural for these statements to evolve over time. For example, Alicia's progression reveals her transition from teaching primarily skills-based undergraduate courses to a range of theory- and research-based courses at both the undergraduate and graduate level. In the early days of teaching, her philosophy reflected a coaching metaphor, with her role as a mentor encouraging her students to develop their personal growth through interpersonal communication and public speaking courses. When Alicia was awarded the Teaching Excellence Award from Southern Illinois University Edwardsville in 2009, she was asked to speak to students and faculty with a panel of past winners about her approach to teaching and learning. During that time she began to reflect on her current philosophy. Using a quotation from one her favorite textbooks, *Intimate Relationships*, by relational scholar Sharon Brehm, she built her philosophy around this statement: "When it comes to relationships, we are all embarked on a lifelong voyage of discovery." To Alicia, this notion of relationship is important because she has found that a great deal of her teaching and mentoring is about fostering healthy relationships. Furthermore, just like relationships, teaching is a lifelong voyage of discovery.

A Philosophy of Teaching: Alicia Alexander

"When it comes to relationships, we are all embarked on a lifelong voyage of discovery." — Sharon Brehm, 1992

This is one of my favorite quotes from relationship researcher Sharon Brehm. For me, this nicely sums up my approach to my research and to my teaching. I take a relational perspective in the way that I approach my work. This perspective involves encouraging active participation, motivating students, and adapting to their individual learning styles. It also involves providing a nurturing environment and fostering my students' self-development.

During my eleven years at Southern Illinois University Edwardsville (SIUE), I have taught fourteen different course topics. Teaching this many different classes in such a brief time period has proved to be an interesting, yet challenging, task. From teaching a range of undergraduate and graduate, skills-based and theory-based, lecture-style and seminar-style classes, I have certainly had to adapt my own teaching style to the goals of the course and to the needs of my students. Throughout my courses I strive to provide a nurturing environment, foster self-development, apply and integrate knowledge, and always work to enhance my teaching effectiveness.

Provide a Nurturing Environment. I remember one of my favorite professors once said, "Strong communication skills can open doors." To me, that statement was particularly empowering. I began to understand that learning about communication is essential for succeeding in many areas of life. Since that time, it has become my mission to encourage my students to understand and improve their communication to become more confident and powerful people. One of my goals in teaching communication courses is to serve as a "coach" facilitating my students' learning. In this role I endeavor to provide a nurturing environment and encourage apprenticeship for my students. I often encourage my students' efforts by challenging them while at the same time promoting a climate of caring and trust to help them exceed their own goals. I hope for them to see that their achievement is a product of their own effort and ability. When teaching a course in research methods, a course often feared by new graduate students, I try to take them carefully through each step of the research process until they feel comfortable approaching a project on their own. Further, when working with graduate students on their theses, I am diligent in helping them get organized by setting a detailed calendar for completion. I ensure that they set realistic goals for completing the project. A second dimension of providing a nurturing environment includes developing an apprenticeship. This involves socializing students into new behavioral norms and ways of working. With my graduate students, I try to change and adapt to their needs as they progress through the program to encourage them to develop from dependent learners to independent thinkers.

Foster Self-Development.   One of my primary goals for teaching effectiveness in my classes is to enhance students' self-development. This goal is particularly evident in my Interpersonal Communication Skills course as well as my Advanced Presentations course. Both classes are designed to help students assess their personal strengths and weaknesses in their interpersonal and public communication. In the advanced course, students are asked to watch their recorded performances and provide written self-assessments of their strengths and areas for improvement. I also ask students to perform a "Job Talk" presentation that entails students locating a job of interest and then "interviewing" for this job by presenting their personal strengths and experiences applicable to the job. These two assignments have proved to help students improve their confidence and professionalism, as well as to help them recognize their own potential contributions to the professional world. Many students have commented that they appreciated the extra help in getting a jump on their career goals.

Encourage Problem Solving.   Problem solving is essential for a career path in communication. In my interpersonal and family communication classes many of the lectures and discussions focus on ways for improving communication. In my Family Communication class I offer scenarios of hypothetical and research-generated family communication problems to facilitate class discussion. Students are encouraged to analyze the situation using the concepts and theories they have learned in class. This assignment is particularly useful for helping students develop critical-thinking skills while applying their knowledge to realistic issues. In my Advanced Presentations class I have incorporated a team problem-solving presentation in which students are asked to thoroughly define and analyze a university or St. Louis community problem. Students are then asked to use their creativity and critical-thinking abilities to search out and present well-defined solutions to solve the problem. This project has been useful for encouraging students to develop their persuasive abilities and teamwork skills as well as highlighting the importance of taking responsibility for local issues and serving as engaged citizens.

Apply and Integrate Knowledge.   Another goal of mine is to encourage students to apply their knowledge to real-world problems and issues while developing a critical mind. The major assignment in my Family Communication class requires students to use scholarly research to analyze a popular press self-help book. For example, students may choose John Gray's book *Men Are from Mars, Women Are from Venus* and analyze the book using current research from reputable journals. This assignment is beneficial in helping students learn to organize and synthesize information, develop an acute awareness of ethical and credible works, and apply and assimilate course concepts.

Enhance My Own Teaching Effectiveness.   While I believe that I have several strengths in my teaching ability, I have many goals for enhancing my effectiveness as an instructor and a mentor. Through careful inspection of my teaching evaluations, peer reviews, and interpersonal feedback from my students, I have made efforts to enhance my teaching effectiveness. For instance, I have tried to engage with my students' comments that my "tests are difficult" and "questions can be tricky." While I do not want to sacrifice the importance of rigor or lower my standards, I tried to think of this issue from my students' perspective. I have since offered more thorough review sheets placed on my Blackboard site, and I have requested peer feedback on the questions that I have created. I have also given students sample exam questions to help them become familiar with the format and expectations. Thus, while I have always encouraged self-assessment for my students, I truly believe in the power of self-assessment to improve my own teaching abilities as well. I have learned much from my students and my colleagues through the years and I look forward to growing even more as a teacher and scholar in the coming years. While it takes a lifetime to develop and enhance our interpersonal communication skills, it could also be said, "When it comes to *teaching*, we are all embarked on a lifelong voyage of discovery."

Hopefully, Alicia's philosophy gives you a bit of inspiration for beginning or modifying your existing philosophy. As we stated earlier, the first consideration for any teaching philosophy is to realize that it evolves over time. Second, think of developing and updating your teaching philosophy not as a chore but as an opportunity to be self-reflective. Constantly re-evaluating your own weaknesses, strengths, and goals as an instructor, while focusing on the best ways to meet your students' needs, will help you avoid becoming stale or bored by your own teaching methods. Revising your statement can be a surprising source of inspiration and a refreshed outlook.

Third, utilize the wide variety of resources available to help you develop a statement unique to your beliefs. The teaching and learning centers at most universities provide detailed instructions on how to create a statement and examples from their own teachers. Some of our favorite recommendations are from the University of Minnesota's Center for Teaching and Learning (www1.umn .edu/ohr/teachlearn/tutorials/philosophy/) and the Ohio State University's Center for Teacher Advancement (http://ucat.osu.edu/read/teaching-portfolio /philosophy). These sites also include links to additional resources where you can find more guidance.

PROFESSIONAL DEVELOPMENT

Having an approach to teaching means considering yourself a professional in the classroom and establishing a philosophy that guides your instructional methods. From the point of view of technical expertise, professional development — keeping your skills up and staying current with the trends in the field — is the primary tool for furthering the growth process. In this section we will discuss three recommended avenues for professional development:

- creating and maintaining a teaching portfolio;
- participating in teaching excellence training conducted by your university and the National Communication Association or similar professional organizations; and
- using your own consulting and training opportunities as a mechanism for bringing real-world feedback into the classroom.

Teaching Portfolios

A teaching portfolio is a record of your teaching accomplishments. A portfolio can serve as both a professional development tool and evidence for your own advancement or promotion and tenure. Virtually all instructors in the field of education now maintain teaching portfolios, but it is only recently that instructors of communication have begun to assemble portfolios. In general, a portfolio will

- reflect you as a professional teacher — your philosophy and training as a teacher and some of the experiences you have had over the course of your career;
- serve as a demonstration of your effectiveness as a teacher because evaluations are contained within the portfolio; and
- provide a historical picture of you as a teacher through a chronological record of responsibilities — your past achievements, present activities, and future plans.

Portfolios are ultimately a tool to improve teaching.

There are many books (e.g., Campbell, 2004) and articles (e.g., Quinlin, 2002; Syre & Pesa, 2001) available through your school library that can show you basic standards for setting up a portfolio and thinking about how it will be reviewed by colleagues. Elizabeth's portfolio is based on the criteria of her university's teaching excellence award, and she updates it every summer. The contents include

1. statement of teaching philosophy
2. methods used to achieve educational goals (including sample syllabi, student papers, honors thesis, etc.)
3. teaching goals for the next five years
4. current vita, including list of courses taught and developed at UNCG
5. interdepartmental and interdisciplinary activities related to teaching
6. information documenting advising activities, guided student projects, supervision of honors projects, graduate theses/dissertations
7. letters of teaching effectiveness (peer reviews, letters from students)
8. numerical and descriptive data by students from course evaluations

Other items might be useful in a portfolio: copies of books or articles to accompany the teaching philosophy (item 1 above); coauthored publications with students to support item 6 above; awards received if the portfolio is used for promotion and tenure or a job application; photographs of student activities to enhance items 5 and 6 above; course proposals to support item 4 above; copies of conference or workshop presentations given to demonstrate teaching expertise. You should carefully review your university's expectations as you compile your portfolio. You can find this information in promotion and tenure guidelines and in calls for nominations for teaching awards. Don't wait! Assemble a basic portfolio now and use it to develop professionally throughout your career.

If you are new to teaching you might be thinking, "Portfolio? Start it now? But I don't have time for that!" But we urge you to consider starting your portfolio from your very first teaching experience. As the director and trainer of the teaching assistants in her department, Alicia requires her graduate students to begin their portfolio during their first semester in her Seminar in Communication Education course. She asks her students to get organized right away by carefully filing course lectures, activities, quizzes, and any materials they created for the course. She also encourages the students to take notes throughout the semester on what activities worked or didn't work, and why or why not, as well as discussion questions that seemed to generate lively interaction. Additionally, she prompts her teaching assistants to attend teaching enhancement workshops on campus and to take note of how they implemented the ideas in their courses. Her teaching assistants also work on creating their teaching philosophies in the course. Of course, they often struggle with developing this first draft. But getting your ideas out for the first time can really help frame your current and future teaching. Alicia refers to the teaching philosophy as a "living document" that needs constant updating and reflection to best fit your current teaching beliefs and needs. While it is a lot of work to develop a philosophy and portfolio, many of Alicia's former teaching assistants have commented on how helpful it was for them to have started a portfolio when it came to applying for jobs later.

Keep in mind too that some organizations and universities are interested in digital portfolios as well. We urge you to consider looking into ways to highlight your teaching effectiveness through various digital means. This could be useful because it allows you to use more text, graphics, color, and additional links. Perhaps you could use blog posts as part of your portfolio, online lectures, video-recorded lectures, online discussion posts, a digital dropbox, a Web site, or other creative devices to highlight your teaching experiences. A digital portfolio could be useful as it offers an evolving project that can be easily updated and accessible to multiple audiences.

Professional Organizations

The primary professional organization for communication educators in the United States is the National Communication Association (NCA), founded in 1914. On its Web site homepage (www.natcom.org) the association describes its purpose, in part, by stating: "NCA works with its members to strengthen the profession and contribute to the greater good of the educational enterprise and society." We recommend membership in the NCA as a wise investment in the discipline of communication. When you register, be sure to affiliate with the Interpersonal Communication Division, and possibly the Family

Communication Division, so you receive the newsletter and other information of specific interest to you. The NCA Web site itself is a marvelous resource to help you think about ways to develop professionally. For example, the pull-down menu on the home page labeled Teaching and Learning has several links within the "Virtual Faculty Lounge" that cover topics such as assessment resources, assignment ideas, course teaching tips, and sample syllabi.

The NCA is also the publisher of many journals that offer articles to improve your teaching. For example, *Communication Education* and *Communication Teacher* offer a range of theoretical, research-oriented, and practical pedagogies that can enhance both your knowledge and your skill as a teacher of interpersonal communication. As a communication educator, you can enjoy current knowledge of the field by reading such publications. Select a journal that will enhance your teaching, and make a commitment to yourself to read through four times a year. At a faculty meeting during Elizabeth's first year of teaching, one of her senior colleagues suggested that they all receive their journals at their home addresses. He argued that a person would be more likely to read at home, whereas at the office they might just shelve the journal without taking a significant look. We both have received all our journals at home for many years, and he was right!

Professional organizations offer training in the form of workshops and panels at their annual conventions. We both enjoy attending the Great Ideas for Teaching Speech (GIFTS) panels at the regional and national conferences. Usually these panels consist of a series of short presentations by instructors who teach public speaking, interpersonal communication, or hybrid courses. These practical "gifts" offer creative strategies to make the classroom a better learning site. At NCA you can sign up for short courses on topics relevant to interpersonal communication. Short courses usually run for three hours and often include copies of texts, sample syllabi, and course activities.

Make it a priority to join a state, regional, or national organization as part of your professional development agenda. Go to the annual conferences and subscribe to journals that will broaden your scope and depth of interpersonal communication knowledge. Attend at least one workshop or panel every year and take the suggested activity back into your classroom to try it out.

Training and Consulting

Depending on where you are in the course of your teaching career, you will receive calls to train or consult with agencies and organizations that need help with interpersonal communication problem solving or employee training. About five years into her career Elizabeth started training managers and employees out in the community. For many years she worked with managers in state government and taught a regular interpersonal skills course that constituted about twenty hours of training. For the last several years she has taught a diversity course in a management development program that targets managers in her region of North Carolina. Between the two of us we have worked with corporate managers, churches, hospital social workers, city employees, student officers in university organizations, attorneys, university faculty and staff, speech and hearing clinicians, employees at an insurance company, and employees of the federal judiciary. Because we take interpersonal concepts, skills, and theories out into the community, we have a strong knowledge of how the interpersonal communication process works in the real world. It's like a testing ground to see if what we are teaching our students has applicability beyond the classroom. At the same time, we bring the concerns and issues of our students' future employers back into the classroom. The back-and-forth between our students and our clients is an excellent way to teach information that is up-to-date and practical. Our own professional development is enhanced through these training and consulting opportunities, and we are ultimately better teachers. We encourage you to take advantage of such opportunities when they come your way. Think through your expertise and how you will respond when you receive your first call from a community agency. What can you do and, just as important, what can you *not* do? If you are a senior professor, invite younger colleagues to go with you as a co-trainer so they can see firsthand how beneficial such opportunities are.

COMING TO CLOSURE ON EFFECTIVE TEACHING . . . FOR NOW

Some people think good teaching is a knack — that we come to it naturally if we are good at it. Maybe there is a "teacher personality," and those of us with such a personality gravitate toward the profession. We agree with Bill Rawlins (2000) and Peter Filene (2005) that teaching is inherently relational and that effective teachers bring a philosophical orientation on relationships and teaching when they enter the interpersonal communication classroom. This chapter highlighted some of these philosophical characteristics by looking at the thoughts of professors in both education and communication. If you are a new teacher, make a list now of key phrases and concepts that you perceive to be core components in your teaching philosophy.

_____   _____
_____   _____
_____   _____

Over the next several months, craft a written statement that will guide you more effectively and that you can have as part of your teaching portfolio. If you are a seasoned teacher, take out your statement of teaching philosophy now and review it. Make amendments as appropriate. No matter where you are in your career, you have to love students and the learning process for this career to mean something to everyone involved.

SETTING GOALS

Now is the time to set goals for your own development as a teacher of interpersonal communication. To assist, we will outline possible areas of goal consideration. Depending on where you are in your career, your goals should reflect a logical point for improving your teaching. For example, do you have knowledge-based goals? ("My goal is to develop a deeper knowledge of the conflict literature to close a gap in my teaching on that interpersonal topic.") Do you have philosophical goals? ("My goal is to commit a philosophy of teaching to paper so I can use that philosophy to be a better teacher of interpersonal communication.") Perhaps you have technical goals. ("My goal is to take a professional development workshop on interpersonal communication to help me manage my classroom more effectively.") Knowing that you cannot set and reach multiple goals overnight, prioritize your goals as short-term or long-term. Decide for yourself what *short* and *long* mean. Try to be as specific as possible so that you can be realistic in goal setting.

Short-term Goals

Goal #1: _____

_____

Strategy to reach goal #1: _____

_____

Goal #2: _____

_____

Strategy to reach goal #2: _____

_____

Long-term Goals

Goal #1: _____

_____

Strategy to reach goal #1: _____

_____

Goal #2: _____

_____

Strategy to reach goal #2: _____

_____

Review these goals and strategies at the beginning and end of each semester. Make changes as appropriate. Discuss your progress with colleagues or a mentor. On a separate page, develop a unified plan for professional development by outlining what you've read about in this chapter: strengths, challenges, teaching philosophy, goals, and strategies. This plan will help you stay on the path of professionalism and effectiveness. To help you gain more insight into what really works in the interpersonal classroom, the next four chapters reveal helpful information on constructing a syllabus, managing the classroom, dealing with student problems, developing instructional strategies, and implementing a system for evaluating student work.

2

The Basic Tool of Effective Teaching: The Syllabus

The syllabus is the backbone of the interpersonal communication course. Without this fundamental skeletal component, the course would not work. A syllabus links teacher and student so they can effectively manage and accomplish the course objectives. In this chapter we will look at the function of a syllabus. We will then dissect a sample syllabus, reviewing the scope of the course, the learning objectives, the organization of course content, and how supporting materials enhance a syllabus. Finally, we will discuss variations on a syllabus, depending on course needs such as emphasizing theory or focusing on service learning. After reading this chapter you should be able to construct a syllabus that will serve as a strong foundation for your introductory course and help you be a more effective teacher.

THE FUNCTION OF A SYLLABUS

A syllabus serves several purposes, all of which are interconnected. The primary function of a syllabus is to organize the course so that learning can be successful. The syllabus delivers essential information to help the student navigate the course. The organization outlined serves as a study guide when students prepare for examinations. The syllabus also functions as a policy document because it typically contains important protocol about attendance, the implementation of exams, grading, and other departmental and university policies. Finally, the syllabus is a legal document that binds professor and student in contractual agreement. All of these functions are interconnected because technical, legal, and pedagogical details are needed in the learning environment. Even so, as suggested by L. B. Curzon, "above all, the teacher's own interpretation of the learner's needs at his or her current stage of development" (2004, p. 189) is what should underlie the syllabus. This is good advice and keeps you on track in your job as the instructor. In her compact and useful book titled *The Course Syllabus: A Learning-Centered Approach*, Judith Grunert (1997) lists sixteen functions of a syllabus that include everything from setting the tone of the course to communicating the role of technology — all of which aid the educational development of the student. Look at Table 2.1 and see if these functions sound reasonable to you.

Because students tend not to read a syllabus thoroughly or understand how much it can contribute to student success (in fact, first-year students in college

TABLE 2.1. Judith Grunert's 16 Functions of a Learning-Centered Syllabus

---

1. Establishes an early point of contact and connection between student and instructor.
2. Helps set the tone for your course.
3. Describes your beliefs about educational purposes.
4. Acquaints students with the logistics of the course.
5. Contains collected handouts.
6. Defines student responsibilities for successful course work.
7. Describes active learning.
8. Helps students to assess their readiness for your course.
9. Sets the course in a broader context for learning.
10. Provides a conceptual framework.
11. Describes available learning resources.
12. Communicates the role of technology in the course.
13. Can expand to provide difficult-to-obtain reading materials.
14. Can improve the effectiveness of student note taking.
15. Can include material that supports learning outside the classroom.
16. Can serve as a learning contract.

From Judith Grunert (1997). *The Course Syllabus: A Learning-Centered Approach* (pp. 14–19). Bolton, MA: Anker Publishing.

may be seeing a syllabus for the first time), you should go over the syllabus on the first day of class. It is tempting to rush through the syllabus on the first day to get to the "fun stuff," like icebreakers, but we suggest that you give ample time to discuss all sections of your syllabus. While some students might think that the first class period will be short, taking the time to cover every aspect of the syllabus ensures everyone is clear on the expectations of the course. Be sure to ask several questions throughout your discussion of the syllabus to encourage an environment of questioning and to make sure everyone understands your expectations. Then, you can begin the second day of the semester with this invitation: "Now that you've had time to review the syllabus and think about what's ahead this semester, do you have any questions about the syllabus or the course?" There is usually at least one question.

It is also important to note that you can place your syllabus, course calendar, and course packet online before your course begins. This gives students the opportunity to get familiar with the course in advance. In fact, many of Alicia's colleagues at SIUE have opted to place their course materials *only* online on Blackboard and request that students in face-to-face courses print the materials in advance or bring a device for reading the online content in class. Students are also asked to come prepared with questions. This cuts down on the cost of copying and wasted paper as many students are ready to pull up the syllabus on their laptops, smartphones, or tablets. However, we recommend that you have the syllabus ready on PowerPoint or other display methods in the event that some students do not have technology for viewing the materials.

To counteract casual student attitudes about the role of the syllabus, we emphasize our use of the document throughout the semester. A tightly structured syllabus helps us implement the various functions of information delivery, policy archive, semester organization, and study guide for exams. After all, as educator Ruby Higgins argues, the syllabus is "an aspect of the instructor's role of communicator" (1994, p. 408). And now that technology makes it easy for students to always access or reprint syllabi, the most common complaint — "I lost my syllabus" — no longer stands as a valid reason for a student's falling behind.

Overall, a syllabus should align with your teaching approach. For example, if you have a skills-based course, the syllabus should make that clear. Also, check that it organizes the semester accordingly. The same criteria apply to all types of courses, such as service learning–based courses or online courses. A student or a peer instructor reviewing your syllabus should be able to locate in the document the purpose of the course, stated learning objectives, class schedule, and any description of activities related to the course. Why is this important? A straightforward statement of approach tells everyone in the learning community where they are going and what they are striving to achieve. For example, if you are teaching a skills-based course, a student should be able to see that certain skills need to be learned and that those skills will support enhanced interpersonal communication in the real world. In fact, a skills-based approach is the most common scope of an entry-level interpersonal communication course.

Generally, most courses are tied to textbooks that teach skills based in research and theory. If, however, the course serves a research function or a service-learning function as part of the departmental curriculum, then it is a good idea to make that clear on the syllabus so that your students have some context for the course. In our departments, our introductory interpersonal course is also a required core course that supports the department's mission statement. On Elizabeth's syllabus, she makes it clear to the students that the course fulfills a role in delivering the relationships component of the mission statement: "We teach the strategic and ethical uses of communication to build relationships and communities."

THE ELEMENTS OF A SYLLABUS

While doing research for this chapter, we examined many different syllabi from introductory interpersonal communication courses. Although we found many similarities among the syllabi, each still reflected the unique teaching style of its respective instructor — proof that there is no single correct way to structure a syllabus. Most instructors tend to order a syllabus with access information first, followed by learning objectives, policies, assignments, and a daily schedule. This organization may reflect more custom than pedagogical logic, but the end result should be clear information that guides the student through the course. Communication pedagogy expert Jean Civikly-Powell (1999) advocates that a syllabus has two good payoffs: to reduce "student uncertainty and anxiety about the course and expectations for successful performance" (p. 70) and to serve as "the all-in-one-place reference manual" (p. 70) to reduce class time spent on procedural issues. Such payoffs are well worth the time you will invest in constructing a syllabus.

We now share with you the syllabus that Alicia created for her own introductory interpersonal communication course. Let's examine it carefully and dissect the basic elements. If you are an experienced instructor, you may want to compare yours with this one to see if it sparks any new ideas; remember, however, that it is just one example of how a syllabus might be structured.

First note the basic elements of the syllabus: course title, professor access, course purpose/learning objectives, textbook and supply information, course policies (attendance, behavior, exams, homework, honor code, and grading), and the daily schedule. Try to be succinct and complete. Some syllabi may include university policies concerning students with disabilities, class rules for participation or behavior, a statement of prerequisites, or written instructions for specific assignments throughout the course. The "reference manual" approach advocated by Civikly-Powell (1999) means that a syllabus could be ten pages or more by the time it is finished. However, others, such as Ruby Higgins (1994), administrator and former dean at Grambling State University, suggest that a syllabus be no more than three pages long so that students do not suffer from information overload. It is your decision how to honor university, departmental, and personal policies and preferences, but rarely do we see three-page syllabi these days. Check with your department, college, and university to determine if there are any mandated policies such as penalties for missing the first class, general attendance policies, grade reconsideration, and so forth. Alicia's university has a mandated disability policy as well as a departmental policy for classroom civility.

You can supplement a syllabus with a course packet, as we both do. Our packets contain detailed assignment instructions, handouts, class exercises, and an extra copy of the syllabus that we post on Blackboard so that students can have access to these course materials at all times. Further, we recommend that you place the grading rubric for each assignment in the course packet so that students can see in advance the point values for various components of the assignment. Information such as page length required and number of source citations required is helpful on the rubric. Going over the rubric in advance of the assignment relieves some of the students' anxiety about your expectations and can increase the quality of students' work. Although a course packet can take the dramatic suspense out of class discussions because some students have looked ahead, the fact that such a resource is available makes it worth having. Alicia has also noted that having a course packet can prevent you from serving as the constant "taskmaster" with repeated questions such as "How long are our presentations?" and "Can we use online sources?" and so forth.

Although we do not include a teaching philosophy per se on the syllabus, we attempt to enact our philosophy every day in class. We have seen syllabi on which a teaching philosophy is stated briefly, but we are more likely to see statements that invite students to participate in class discussions and/or activities, or that indicate something about the positive communication climate created

by the instructor. We have also read syllabi that presented a potentially negative learning environment by using "dos and don'ts" as the approach for rules
and policies. Granted, the tone in our own syllabi is much firmer than when
we first started teaching many years ago. One reason for this change is that
we feel the need to respond to a student population that, over the years, has
actually become less respectful of both classroom and peers. Our policies on
in-class behavior, for example, may at first seem quite negative. However, if
you examine it carefully you'll see that there is some humanity implicit in the
policy.

SAMPLE SYLLABUS FOR AN ENTRY-LEVEL INTERPERSONAL COMMUNICATION COURSE

Interpersonal Communication Skills

SPC 103

Dr. Alicia Alexander

Office:

Office Phone:

E-mail:

Office Hours:

"When it comes to relationships, we are all embarked on a lifelong voyage of discovery." – Sharon Brehm (1992)

COURSE GOALS

The major aims of this course are to make you a more effective communicator. In this class we will focus on communication in relationships with others such as friends, romantic partners, family members, and coworkers. The goals of this course are to help you: (1) understand and apply key concepts and processes in interpersonal communication, (2) develop an understanding of scholarly research in the field of interpersonal communication, and (3) analyze and improve your interpersonal communication skills.

TEXT

McCornack, S. (2013). *Reflect and relate: An introduction to interpersonal communication* (3rd ed.). Boston: Bedford/St. Martin's.

ASSIGNMENTS

Weekly Insight and Action Papers (40 Points Total):

This assignment is due eight times throughout the semester (see dates on course calendar). These papers will not be accepted after the first 10 minutes of class.

Insight: You will be asked to write about two insights discovered from class lectures, group discussions, and text concepts from the previous week. Think of insights as interesting discoveries, tidbits, or "ah-ha moments."

Action: You must do/say something that will address an attitude or behavior regarding your new insight on interpersonal communication. You need to write about an action for both of your insights. I want to know what you have done or will do to improve this aspect of your interpersonal communication. For example, let's say you heard a student in class say something particularly useful about managing conflict with friends. Following that class you had a conversation with your roommate about your class discussion. You and your roommate talked about ways to improve some recent problems you have been having with conflict over your messy apartment. I want to hear about the results of this conversation and how the course concepts/discussion actually impacted your conflict-resolution skills and relationship with your roommate.

Daily Insight and Action Papers: On Tuesdays you will need to turn in your insights and actions in a **1-page typed** paper (1½ max). Please organize and label your paper into four separate paragraphs for each (i.e., insight #1, action #1, insight #2, action #2).

Oral Reports of Insight and Action: In addition to gaining understanding of your relationships through writing about your insights, you will also have the chance to learn from hearing other classmates' insights. **Each Tuesday** during the first 15 minutes of class the entire class will very briefly share one Insight and Action with the class. Notice that for these oral reports in class, you'll need to be able to follow this 'short' format:

The Insight I had was . . .   **The Action I took was . . .**

At the end of the semester you will report insights from the entire class and provide a longer-lasting goal or action that you plan to accomplish in the future as a result of taking this class.

Participation Points (35 Points): A significant amount of the learning in this course is done by you through discussion, observation, and evaluation of in-class exercises. You will learn communication skills by practicing them with your classmates. In class, you are expected to participate in discussion, pop quizzes, and other activities. You must *participate* in class to receive *participation* points. You may also be asked to complete additional written work and other related exercises outside of class. No makeups will be granted for participation activities.

Team Presentation (45 Points): As a team, you will facilitate a class session on a communication concept in one of the following types of relationships: friends, lovers, coworkers, or family members. Early in the semester you will be assigned to your team. While you will be assigned a particular relationship type for your team, it is up to your team members to determine what communication topic you will be discussing. For example, one team may discuss self-disclosure in friendship relationships while another team may discuss secrets in family relationships. Once you have decided on your topic, your team will need to research the topic you have chosen (you will need to consult additional resources beyond your course textbook). Your job is then to facilitate a learning session on the topic. You must choose some type of interactive activity such as role-plays, discussion questions, small groups, props, and other creative devices to get the class engaged in learning. You will be graded as a team on content, organization, creativity, delivery, and teamwork. You will be required to submit a handout for your presentation that will be distributed to the class on the day of the presentation. This handout should include an overview of your presentation, a bibliography, and three to five exam questions covering your presentation that could be included on your final exam. This assignment is worth a total of 45 points: 40 points for the presentation and 5 points for the handout. Note: All team members will receive the same grade.

Exams (60 Points Each): There will be three exams during the course of the semester. Refer to the course schedule for quiz times and material covered. Your third exam is during the final exam period on Wednesday, December 12, 8:00–9:40. Exams will be made up of multiple-choice, matching, true-false, and short answer items. Each exam is worth 60 points.

Extra Credit: We feel it is important to your education that you experience the kinds of events and research that are critical to our University's mission. Thus, you will be given 2 points of extra credit for each activity you complete with a maximum of 4 points. *If* these opportunities become available, they will be announced in class. They are on a first-come, first-served basis.

GRADING

Grades are determined on a straight percentage scale based on the number of points earned out of a maximum of 300 points. There will be no further rounding or curving of grades. Final grades are calculated as follows:

A = 90%–100%   (270–300)
B = 80%–89.9%   (240–269)
C = 70%–79.9%   (210–239)
D = 60–69.9%   (180–209)
F = below 59.9%   (179 and below)

Use the following chart to keep track of your grades.

ASSIGNMENT	MAXIMUM POINTS POSSIBLE	MY POINTS
Insight and Action #1	5	
Insight and Action #2	5	
Insight and Action #3	5	
Insight and Action #4	5	
Insight and Action #5	5	
Insight and Action #6	5	
Insight and Action #7	5	
Final Insight and Action #8	5	
Participation (*quizzes, homework, group exercises, etc.*)	35 points	
Team Presentation	45 points	
Exam Part One	60 points	
Exam Part Two	60 points	
Exam Part Three	60 points	
Optional Extra Credit (no more than 2)	*4 points max (2 points each)*	
TOTAL COURSE POINTS	300 points	

COURSE POLICIES

Attendance: Because a large portion of the learning in this course occurs during class discussion and activities, your attendance is very important. You are allowed 2 "free" absences. You do not have to clear these 2 absences with me or tell me why. Thus, you should use these "free" absences wisely. Each additional unexcused absence will result in 15 points deducted from your total course grade. Be sure to sign in on the attendance sheet each day. If you are more than 15 minutes late or if you leave at least 15 minutes early, you will be counted absent. Please talk to me promptly in the case of extreme documented situations.

Students who have 5 absences (including the 2 "free" absences) will need to withdraw from the course. The grade that appears on your transcript after withdrawal depends on the week in the semester when the withdrawal occurs. Within the first 10 weeks of the semester, if the student initiates a withdrawal, a "W" will be assigned. After the tenth week and until the last day of the semester, if the student initiates a withdrawal, a "WP" or "WF" will appear, depending on the student's grade in the class at the time of withdrawal. It is the student's responsibility to keep track of his/her absences. If the student fails to withdraw him/herself from the class, the faculty member will initiate the withdrawal and a "UW" will be assigned. Note: It is in the student's interest to initiate the withdrawal process since a "UW" counts as an F on your transcript.

Don't miss class on a day you are scheduled to speak. Please realize that our busy course schedule does not allow flexibility in rescheduling presentations. **Unexcused absences on presentation OR exam days will earn a grade of zero; no makeups will be granted. If a team member or partner is missing, the presentation must go on. The absent member will receive a zero (other members will still present and receive their points).** Absences *may* be excused with **PRIOR** notification in *extreme* situations. You have three means for contacting me for your absence — e-mail, phone, and a visit to my office.

Deadlines are listed in your course schedule and will be announced by your instructor. Assignments must be turned in at the beginning of class on the day they are due. Assignments turned in after class on the due date are considered late. Late written assignments will be penalized 15% of the total points for each day that you are late. No assignments will be accepted two days beyond the due date.

Changes to the schedule may be made at your instructor's discretion and if circumstances require. It is your responsibility to note these changes when announced.

Readings must be completed **on the day they are assigned** on the course schedule. Lectures are intended to *complement* (not duplicate) information provided in the readings.

Written work must be typed. Failure to type any written portion of an assignment results in a 20% point deduction off the total point value of that assignment.

Classroom Civility: People and ideas must be treated with respect. While freedom of speech is an important privilege, it is also important that we create a safe environment for all individuals in this class. Please avoid disruptive behavior that makes it difficult to accomplish our mutual objectives. **Turn off cell phones or other noisy devices before entering the classroom.** You will be asked to leave and will be counted as absent if you are texting or checking Facebook during class. **Laptops, tablets, and cell phones are not allowed during lecture.**

We want to build a sense of classroom community and an atmosphere that is comfortable for all. In a communication class it is especially important that we

- display respect for all in the classroom community (students and the instructor);
- pay attention to and participate in all class sessions, activities, and presentations;
- avoid unnecessary disruption during class time including ringing cell phones, text messaging, playing computer games, private conversations, reading the newspaper, or doing work for other classes (laptops are to be used for class notes ONLY);
- avoid repeatedly blurting out comments or dominating conversations and class lectures; and
- avoid racist, sexist, homophobic, or other negative language that may unnecessarily exclude members of our campus and classroom community.

This is not an exhaustive list of behaviors; rather, they represent the minimal standards that help make the classroom a pleasant place for all concerned and a safe learning environment. Students will be removed from the course in extreme cases.

<u>Academic Integrity</u>: University standards regulating academic integrity (e.g., cheating, plagiarism, etc.) are strictly enforced. **Plagiarism** is a serious offense in this course. Using the words and ideas of others is borrowing something from those individuals. It is always necessary to identify the original source of supporting information; you must cite the source of any material, quoted or paraphrased, used in your presentations. The absence of this documentation constitutes *plagiarism* — a serious academic and professional offense. Proper documentation requires a bibliography of any outside texts you have consulted including both traditional sources and online sources. Be careful to document sources within your presentation outline and bibliography as well as orally during your presentation. Merely restating another individual's ideas in different words does not make the ideas yours. <u>Serious infractions of these rules will result in a failing grade in the course.</u> These standards may seem subtle, so feel free to ask if you have questions or concerns.

<u>Evaluations</u>: Near the end of this course you will be asked to complete an anonymous departmental course evaluation inviting your opinions about the course and my teaching. All responses will be carefully reviewed, though they will be unavailable to me until after final grades have been submitted.

<u>Disabilities</u>: Please talk to me as soon as possible if you have a disability that will impair your ability to participate in this class. I would be happy to meet with you during office hours to discuss how we can work together to accommodate your needs.

Interpersonal Communication Skills: SPC 103
Tentative Course Schedule
Online Reading: Additional readings are available on our course Blackboard site. Your instructor reserves the right to change any part of the course based upon students' progress in this class or other considerations. Any changes to this course schedule or to the syllabus itself will be announced in class.

DAY/DATE	READING	ASSIGNMENTS AND DUE DATES
PART 1: INTERPERSONAL ESSENTIALS		
Week 1: 8/21 & 8/23	Ch 1: Introducing Interpersonal Communication	
Week 2: 8/28 & 8/30	Ch 2: Considering Self	Form Presentation Teams: These will be your groups for activities throughout the semester and for your Team Presentation.
Week 3: 9/4 & 9/6	Ch 3: Perceiving Others	Insight and Action #1 Due 9/4
Week 4: 9/11 & 9/13	Ch 4: Experiencing & Expressing Emotions	Insight and Action #2 Due 9/11
Week 5: 9/18 & 9/20	Finish Emotions and Prepare for Exam	**EXAM ONE 9/20**

PART 2: INTERPERSONAL COMPETENCE		
Week 6: 9/25 & 9/27	Ch 5: Listening Actively	
Week 7: 10/2 & 10/4	Ch 6: Communicating Verbally	Insight and Action #3 Due 10/2
Week 8: 10/9 & 10/11	Ch 7: Communicating Nonverbally	Insight and Action #4 Due 10/9
Week 9: 10/16 & 10/18	Ch 8: Managing Conflict and Power	Insight and Action #5 Due 10/16 Paragraph Description of Team Project Due
Week 10: 10/23 & 10/25	Managing Conflict and Power Continued	Insight and Action #6 Due 10/23

Week 11: 10/30 & 11/1	Preparing for the Group Presentation: Group Communication and Public Speaking Online Reading TBA	**EXAM TWO 11/1**

PART 3: INTERPERSONAL RELATIONSHIPS		
Week 12: 11/6 & 11/8	Ch 9: Relationships with Romantic Partners	
Week 13: 11/13 & 11/15	Ch 10: Relationships with Family Ch 11: Relationships with Friends	Insight and Action #7 Due 11/13 Outline of Team Project Due: One per group through e-mail by 5:00 (aalexan@siue.edu)
Week 14: 11/20 & 11/22	Thanksgiving Week: No Class	
Week 15: 11/27 & 11/29	Ch 12: Relationships in the Workplace	Final Insight and Action #8 Due 11/27 **Team Presentations 11/29 Family Relationships**
Week 16: 12/4 & 12/6		**Team Presentations 12/4 Coworker Relationships 12/4 Marital Relationships 12/6 Dating Relationships 12/6 Friendship Relationships**

Finals week EXAM THREE Wed., Dec 12, 8:00–9:40

Learning Outcomes

Learning outcomes are the skeletal structure of the syllabus; they comprise the actual foundation for the course in interpersonal communication. A professor sets the learning outcomes and then provides a learning environment in which those outcomes can be achieved. All course activities and materials support the expected outcomes, and the syllabus must reflect the choices made to match activities and materials with outcomes. There is no magic number when it comes to how many objectives should be on a syllabus. We've seen no outcomes stated when a course purpose seems to indicate what is expected from student learning, and we've seen as many as a dozen learning outcomes. Be sure there is a logical connection between the learning outcomes specified and all that follows. When you think about students taking five classes per semester, it starts to become unrealistic to think that a student could achieve as many as ten learning outcomes per course and retain what is learned. Be reasonable in your expectations. Just like a parsimonious theory, craft the smallest number of learning outcomes to achieve the most effective results for the body of knowledge under study.

Elizabeth first learned about learning outcomes in an undergraduate education course she was taking on how to construct behavioral objectives, examinations, and other assignments. They used a great book called *Behavioral Objectives and Instruction* (Kibler, Barker, & Miles, 1970) that taught them how to write behavioral objectives based on the work of Benjamin Bloom. Originally offered in 1956, Bloom's famous taxonomy of educational objectives and his six categories of cognition have been the mainstay for teaching aspiring professors how to write statements of expected learning outcomes. (Note that the original term was *behavioral objective*. We now say *learning outcome* to better reflect that what we are trying to teach can have cognitive as well as emotional results. You will hear both phrases used interchangeably.) Bloom outlined an ascending order of six cognitive domains: *knowledge, comprehension, application, analysis, synthesis,* and *evaluation*. These domains are intended to propel a student forward on his or her mastery of a discipline. The absolute beauty of this taxonomy is that it provides a way for the professor to write learning outcomes, as well as to set up course activities and exams appropriate to the cognitive level of the expected outcomes. For example, take a look at the basic student objectives for Elizabeth's course:

1. Define and use a vocabulary of relational communication terms.
2. Apply major theoretical concepts in the field of relational communication to real-world relationships.
3. Analyze his or her own role in interpersonal relationships in a family, professional, friendship, interracial/intercultural, or intimate context.
4. Apply both practical and theoretical knowledge to increase his or her own competency in relational communication skills.
5. Evaluate the effectiveness of an interpersonal relationship.

She used the verb forms of Bloom's taxonomy in writing the objectives in items 2, 3, 4, and 5. Knowledge is the first domain in Bloom's taxonomy; therefore, she made defining terms the first and lowest level of expected cognitive mastery. She uses the vocabulary of interpersonal communication every day in class so that students become familiar with terms such as *dyad, self-disclosure, social exchange,* and *dialectics*; she engages students in vocabulary activities (e.g., *let's construct a Johari Window to see what the implications are for your self-disclosure with your mom*); and she tests vocabulary on an exam by using something as simple as a matching exercise of terms and definitions.

Untrained instructors who teach entry-level classes often set the expected outcomes at the level of application or below. But once you know Bloom's taxonomy, you can stretch yourself and write learning outcomes that push the student toward higher levels of cognition. In real life, for example, we need to *apply* communication skills in dyads, but we will also need to know how to *evaluate* the effectiveness of the relationships in which we participate if those relationships are to grow and remain healthy. An introductory course can achieve both expected outcomes with the right learning outcomes, such as Elizabeth did in learning outcomes 4 and 5 on her syllabus.

David Krathwohl, a collaborator of Bloom's from the beginning, recently described a revised version of Bloom's taxonomy that he developed with some new colleagues (Anderson & Krathwohl, 2001; Krathwohl, 2002). The taxonomy still contains six cognitive dimensions, but there are changes as noted in Table 2.2. The *synthesis* category has been dropped and a *creative* category added. In addition, verbs replace nouns as the names of the categories.

Elizabeth can see the creative category of knowledge at work in one of her colleague's interpersonal courses. He requires students to create a working relationship with someone in the class whom they do not know in order to practice interpersonal skills and to generate activities for themselves and other classmates. Toward the end of the semester the dyads evaluate how well they achieved their assignments together. Using the Bloom and the revised Krathwohl taxonomies will improve both your effectiveness as an instructor and your ability to create the *appropriate* learning outcomes to serve your course and your students' needs.

In planning your learning outcomes, you may need to conform to a departmental syllabus or to the expectations of "marker" courses such as speaking or writing intensives. Elizabeth's syllabus demonstrates two outcomes related to writing, and they follow the objectives of our university-wide program to improve writing. A departmental syllabus may already have learning outcomes specified. Using your own professional judgment and range of academic freedom, be sure that those outcomes honor the learning situation as you see it and that you can teach within its boundaries.

TABLE 2.2 A Comparison of Bloom's Taxonomy and Krathwohl's Revised Taxonomy

Bloom's Taxonomy	Krathwohl's Revised Taxonomy
Knowledge	Remember
Comprehension	Understand
Application	Apply
Analysis	Analyze
Synthesis	Evaluate
Evaluation	Create

In addition to designing learning outcomes that satisfy course, student, and departmental needs, you may also need to conform to assessment expectations. Although the assessment movement has swept the nation since the 1970s (Banta, 2002), many institutions are just now getting on board with it. State legislatures have put much pressure on community colleges and universities to measure learning outcomes on both the level of general education (e.g., writing, reading, critical thinking) and within the disciplines that comprise degree programs (e.g., communication, sociology, etc.). Accrediting agencies, such as the Southern Association of Colleges and Schools (SACS), which serves an eleven-state region, have responded by incorporating evaluation criteria into their accrediting procedures that look at assessment. Institutions that do not demonstrate a systematic approach to an assessment process risk losing accreditation.

Assessment itself is simply the technical process of systematically measuring how well students achieve learning outcomes and then making adjustments to improve the learning environment based on the results of the assessment process. For more than a decade, the National Communication Association has assisted communication professionals in creating learning outcomes and developing assessment procedures (Morreale & Backlund, 1999). If you log on to the NCA Web site at www.natcom.org, click the Teaching and Learning button, and then go to Assessment Resources, you will find three different items to help you set up an assessment plan. You can also attend workshops on the assessment process at NCA, regional, or state professional conferences. Another good source is Linda Suskie's *Assessing Student Learning: A Common Sense Guide* (2004).

While there are many debates and opinions about the validity of assessment, the most important thing you can do is construct your syllabus so that it reflects the demands of your university. The idea behind assessment is to make the learning process better reflect the knowledge and practice of the discipline so that students are better prepared for life. Knowing about learning outcomes, how they link to Bloom's taxonomy, and the state of assessment from a nationwide perspective will help you meet this important challenge effectively and professionally.

Organization of Course Content

Let's now consider the day-to-day content of the course and how that content is posted on the syllabus. In examining syllabi from other instructors, we noticed two commonalities in about 95 percent of them. First, the course content was generally arranged in the same order as the chapters of the textbook in use, and second, the syllabus was structured topically. For instance, the syllabus would start with chapter one of the text and then work its way through the book during the semester. Daily topics followed a progression paralleling the text such as models first, then perception, then language codes, then nonverbal communication, then conflict, and so forth. If you are a novice teacher, it's fine to trust the textbook; after all, textbooks are written by colleagues who have taken on the responsibility of synthesizing the current state of the interpersonal communication scholarship. Popular textbooks in the field tend to systematize the content of what most instructors teach across the country in entry-level courses.

But it isn't only content that is standardized across the field. The most popular structure for an entry-level course is a theory-practice combination in which the instructor introduces theories and concepts from the interpersonal communication scholarship and then has students practice skills that are derived from those theories and concepts. This is why virtually every course covers topics such as self-disclosure and conflict management. Again, this is not a bad thing. However, we'd like to offer you an alternative way of thinking about organizing your course to help your students learn more about the complexities of interpersonal communication.

Return to the last section of Alicia's syllabus and examine the units of instruction and daily assignments. You will see that the course is divided into three total units. The course progression is based on a theory-practice model, but the course reflects a larger philosophy about the nature and function of communication and relationships. Further, the learning outcomes for the course are reflected in the units and assignments as well. Philosophically, we both believe that effective interpersonal relationships are a combination of personal philosophy and the execution of strategies (skills) to achieve a competent dyad.

THEORY-BASED AND SERVICE-LEARNING COURSES

In addition to the common combination theory/practice syllabus, there are other types of introductory interpersonal communication courses, each of which requires a slightly different setup that should be reflected in the syllabus. Visually, a syllabus for a theory-based or service-learning course might look similar to the sample presented in this chapter, but the information will be different to reflect the course approach. In particular, the course descriptions and learning objectives will tip students off as to the specific approach. We'll discuss each of these variations below. However, if you are teaching a completely online interpersonal communication course, see the sample syllabus provided in Chapter 6: Teaching Online Courses in Interpersonal Communication on pages 113–119.

A Theory-Based Syllabus

Theory-based interpersonal communication courses emphasize the theory and research behind the concepts under study and usually aim to teach students basic research procedures. In a theory-based course, the research is combined with experiential activities so the entry-level student is not overwhelmed by theory. The key to a strong theory-based syllabus is to decide if you would like more depth or breadth in the theories you cover. We recommend that you generate a list of "must know" and "nice to know" theories that you believe fit your students' needs. Some instructors choose a "parade of theories" approach that includes one theory per class period. Other instructors choose to provide a snapshot of a few theories within a specific topic for any class period. Try to consider how your students best retain information and how they will use the theories for future endeavors. We recommend that instructors aim for a lot of application of theories through various teaching devices such as role-plays, video clips, personal journal application, and other methods in order to help students understand the complexities of all of the theories. It is also useful to spend time providing an overview of methodological approaches so that students will understand the ways in which theories are developed and revised.

What this all means for your syllabus is that you should clearly lay out emphasis on theory in your learning objective and course requirements sections and, if possible, give a detailed overview of the theories and activities that will be covered in each class period.

A Service-Learning Syllabus

Service-learning courses are becoming more popular across the country and include community service as part of the pedagogy of the course. For an interpersonal communication course, a theme of building effective relationships might be focused on a particular type of relationship, given the community sites available. For example, a nursing home as a community site will focus on college-age students building relationships with senior citizens. Other types of interpersonal relationships that could be the focus of service learning include those with the homeless, children, immigrants, and HIV-positive patients. Appropriate readings and service activities would support the traditional texts and activities found in an interpersonal communication course. The syllabus will need to reflect all of this by adding appropriate information to the descriptions of course purpose, objectives, readings, grading, activities, policies, and the calendar. Service-learning courses usually require ten to twenty hours of on-site participation in addition to regular classroom meetings. If your university has a service-learning office, consult them for policies and procedures that affect the information needed on a syllabus because there are sometimes legal requirements that need to be incorporated.

The important thing to remember is that your syllabus must reflect the type of course you are offering and the focus of instruction. Students should not be in doubt about what to expect over the course of the semester. The last major issues we need to discuss regarding your choices in constructing the syllabus revolve around supporting materials and textbooks.

SELECTING COURSE MATERIALS

It should be clear by now that logical fit serves as a primary principle for constructing a syllabus. That is, every choice you make to create a learning environment must have a logical fit and be reflected on the syllabus. We have talked about structure, learning outcomes, underlying teacher philosophy and understanding of the field, approach to teaching, assessment, marker courses, and organizational structure as interrelated pieces of a puzzle that must fit together in the end to create a pedagogically sound course. Selecting course materials, however, is actually your biggest responsibility because, for entry-level students, these are the main tools they will rely on day after day to gain knowledge and pass the course.

In today's world, *course materials* can mean many things — the primary textbook, of course, but also the many formats it may be available in, such as loose-leaf, e-book, or custom versions. Then, there is the variety of supporting materials like videos, adaptive quizzing, online activities, or course management systems. All of these materials come together to form the supporting foundation for your course. And, despite students' concern with "Will that be on the test?" your primary goal is to choose materials that best represent the knowledge you want students to obtain during the course. And, if students find these materials accessible and engaging and helpful to using theory and skills in their lives, well then, all the better. With all that in mind, how do you select appropriate course materials, especially the textbook?

Many people use popularity as a criterion for selecting a textbook. What this means is that certain texts gain in use through popularity and thus drive the market. Though, frankly speaking, if you conduct a content analysis of the most popular texts in any field, you will find that about 80 percent of the content is similar. Instructors expect certain theories and concepts (that is, "the accepted knowledge of the field") to be present in the text. The other 20 percent of textbook content varies based on author preference and knowledge and what a publisher wishes to do in a particular niche.

When selecting a textbook, ask yourself these three questions:

1. Is the course skill-based, theory-based, relationship-/context-based, or a combination?
2. What are the reading comprehension abilities of my students?
3. What is the typical age of my students?

Then, consider the following checklist. You may not agree with all the criteria, but the list offers a starting point. Note that popularity is not our first criterion, but it does have a place in overall decision making. We developed this list from both experience and our work in synthesizing the literature on college teaching. The first criterion is the most important and implies that your view of interpersonal communication matches the view of the textbook author.

_____ The textbook meets the needs of the learning outcomes established for the course.

_____ The majority of chapters in the textbook will be used as required reading to support the learning environment.

_____ The textbook is well received by the students for its legibility and usefulness.

_____ The reading level is appropriate for students' average comprehension level — that is, it is neither too difficult nor too simplistic.

_____ The textbook contains activities, discussion questions, and other prompts that inspire the learning process.

_____ The textbook contains enough mainstream and current knowledge to get the student on par with other entry-level students across the communication field.

_____ The supporting materials that come with the textbook are useful to your instruction (e.g., online video supplements, discussion questions, weblinks, multimedia presentations, exam question generators).

_____ The textbook is affordable in the context of the textbook market and your university bookstore policies.

Once you have selected the textbook, you need to make decisions about other supporting materials. Most textbooks do not cover all the reading you need a student to do in order to achieve the learning outcomes. For theory-based courses you may want to require your students to have access to the latest version of the _American Psychological Association (APA) Style Guide_ for writing tips and citation information. Other supporting materials may include publisher-provided Web sites, adaptive quizzing software, videos, or other online activities; PowerPoint or Prezi slides developed by you or the publisher; instructional resources, such as Instructor Manuals or Test Banks; films to be viewed during or outside of class; materials for activities in class; and guest speakers. Note that technical supplies support instruction, but they are quite different from items such as movies. You must think on several levels about how materials support instruction. Index cards for use in class activities are part of the ease of instructional delivery, while movies are carefully selected because they assist in the delivery of concepts. It may take some time in the classroom before you know which supporting materials work best, and even then it is a constant responsibility to update materials in order to relate to student knowledge and social positioning. For example, when it comes to romantic comedies that teach about gender, romance, and interpersonal communication, as much as previous generations loved _Seinfeld_ and _Friends_, we find that today's students relate better to _The Big Bang Theory_ and reality TV shows. Think about what works for you, your students, and the concept under study. Make a list of both technical and pedagogical supporting materials for yourself and your students, and then plug those materials into the syllabus as needed.

LEGIBILITY AND DESIGN

We will end this chapter with a note on syllabus legibility and design. Make your best effort to be clear, readable, and professional. Leave enough white space for students to see sections of the syllabus and make notes. We have seen any number of syllabi with cut-and-paste artwork that is cute, but may be distracting. While it is important to have your own style represented on the syllabus, keep in mind that any additional material should directly relate to the course and should not diminish the importance of the content. Although the use of designs, cartoons, figures, and even photographs on a syllabus is up to the instructor, our advice is to present a professional document where graphics serve only to support the information given. Alicia often places one of her favorite quotations at the top of the syllabus that directly relates to the course material. For example, in her family communication course her syllabus states a quotation from Sharon Brehm's text: "When it comes to relationships, we are all embarked on a lifelong voyage of discovery." While this is a quote that frames her teaching philosophy, it also starts off the first mini-lecture on the importance of enhancing family communication. You can add your own personal flair to your course materials without losing professionalism or distracting your students. Thus, additional material should be related, be useful, and help set the tone of the course.

What new ideas do you want to try out in constructing or revising your interpersonal communication course syllabus? Make notes here:

_____

_____

_____

_____

_____

3

Student Challenges and Problematics

Stepping into the classroom is the best part of our day. We love being with our students. Anything can happen in a given class period, from funny incidents to students turning on each other when they disagree over an issue. You just never know what *could* happen. As experienced teachers, our jobs are to manage the classroom environment and the people in it so that we all work together in a productive and respectful manner. In this chapter we will examine some basic management issues and then move on to discuss disruptive students, nontraditional students, and co-cultural students.

CLASSROOM MANAGEMENT

The most basic aspect of classroom management is organizing people and space. We will talk about space first, but it is important to note that people are part of that space. A traditional face-to-face classroom may have twenty-five to thirty-five students with movable desks — a luxury. This mobility allows you to configure the desks in rows, circles, or small groups to meet the needs of the instructional activity. If the seating arrangement is fixed because the tables or furniture are bolted to the floor, you may have to get creative by moving people rather than furniture, in order for students to get to know each other. But even in an auditorium with one hundred people in the class, we have grouped students together to work. They will often sit on the floor or the stage if they are not comfortable doing group work in their seats. Whatever classroom setup you are given, it is important to remember that it is *your* space and *your* class time. Alicia always encourages her teaching assistants to "own your space" whenever they step into a classroom. That is, instructors have to find a way to make the space work for their teaching goals, whether this includes moving around desks and chairs, adding in a speaker's podium, or bringing in your own large Post-it notes for groupwork and brainstorming. You just need to remember to have proper classroom etiquette and return the classroom to its original form, erase the board, and so forth before you leave.

Many communication professors are inclined to use circles because they believe circles promote face-to-face interaction. We have found them to be limiting, and those limits correspond to the number of people you are trying to fit into a circle in a fixed amount of space. In our experience thirty-five people don't fit in a circle very neatly. In order to make all the desks fit, students wind up with their backs shoved up against a wall, and there is no personal space between desks. The huge open space in the middle becomes dead space. Consequently, the teacher has difficulty sitting in a spot that allows him or her to maintain eye contact with all the students; also, there ends up being very little room for instructional equipment. If you need access to the board or multimedia, you wind up sitting near the equipment and getting up and down. If students are late to class, they must cut through the circle to find a seat and disturb whatever discussion is going on. You get the picture. Circles may be ideal for intimate discussion with small numbers of people, but they may not be the best arrangement for daily large-class interaction. One solution to the circle is to try a semi-circle or "U-shape" where students can still see the chalkboard or screen. This allows you to move in and out of the "U" for interaction and easily use classroom technology. However, it takes a fairly large classroom for this arrangement to ensure students aren't dealing with the same problems as mentioned above. This is why we believe that rows work best overall. They keep students facing the information on the board or screen, and we are able to make eye contact with each person in a consistent manner. We break off into dyads or groups frequently, so students still have plenty of opportunity for interpersonal interactions as well.

In an auditorium setting, Elizabeth recommends using a seating chart. Students pick a seat after about four class periods together. Each student writes his or her preferred name and seat number on a 3 × 5 card, and the teaching assistant draws up the chart. The TA can quickly take roll and the instructor can learn the names of virtually everyone in the classroom. In a class of more than one hundred students, the psychology of knowing students' names is an amazing teaching strategy. When students think you know them (even if you don't), they are more inclined to come to class and participate. Names actually promote a positive communication climate and make the classroom seem more personal.

Teaching assistants are essential in a large class. It is important to value this relationship as a team effort, and treat your TA as a colleague right from the beginning. Elizabeth starts and ends the semester going out to lunch with her TAs, something she believes is an interpersonal ritual. They confer about every class session beforehand, so they each know what they are doing in advance. Elizabeth lets the TA handle the media, attendance, folders for each student, and exam collation, as well as help with demonstrations. The TA normally teaches at least one class period and sometimes more if he or she is training to be a university professor. We both frequently talk with our TAs about pedagogy and share teaching knowledge with TAs throughout the semester. Our TAs hold office hours and answer a lot of procedural questions from students. The key to a successful relationship is anticipating each other. See the box on page 45 for comments from Julia Wood, at UNC–Chapel Hill, who has her own system for working with TAs to manage the classroom.

Two other basic management devices are worth mentioning here. In a very old-fashioned manner, we pass out 3 × 5 cards on the first day of class and collect the following information from each student: name and preferred nickname, local address and phone, e-mail, year in school and major, interests in communication, and hobbies. This is an amazing amount of information to help us stay in contact with students and get to know them. You can also

---

FROM THE CLASSROOM: The Challenge of a Large Class

For years the biggest challenge for me has been teaching the class as a large class (80 to 150) with recitation sections. I used to teach classes of twenty to thirty in which I knew all of my students and knew many of them quite well. Although I learn the names of students in my large classes, I get to know only a handful of students in each class. That's frustrating to someone like me who believes that the best teaching and learning grow out of relationships.

My effort to meet the challenge has primarily focused on working closely with my teaching team (three to five TAs who meet with recitation sections, which I also visit). I invest a great deal of energy in developing the TAs—a couple of hours every week for team meetings—so that they are effective in their section meetings and so that they develop as teachers in their own right. The professional, pedagogical development that I guide in team meetings is like teaching an extra course—I'm teaching them how to teach by working with them on everything from conceptualizing syllabi to debriefing activities. It's not a perfect solution. It doesn't eliminate the frustration I feel about not knowing all of my students personally. But it does ensure quality teaching in the course and it prepares a next generation of teachers.

Julia Wood
Lineberger Distinguished Professor of Humanities
University of North Carolina at Chapel Hill

SOURCE: Personal correspondence with Elizabeth Natalle, April 27, 2006.

---

manage group or dyad composition by pairing students based on similarities or differences. If your university e-mail system is restricted—that is, you may only contact students based on the university e-mail address—the card contains back-up information. You can keep the cards right by your phone and computer at the office and use them frequently.

In a large class (let's say more than thirty-five), Elizabeth asks each student to bring in a manila folder so she can file exams, assignments, Scantron forms, and other materials. She can carry folders to class using a portable file box on test days, or hand it off to a TA while preparing materials. This system works well and helps to manage paper and people.

If you struggle with learning names, like Elizabeth's colleague David Carlone, here is another idea. David takes a digital camera to class and snaps a photograph of each student. He then puts a name to a photo and studies this in order to learn names more quickly. If you are teaching an online course, having students post a picture with their name can also help everyone meet and get to know each other. Alicia uses another tactic and videorecords her students on the first day of class by asking students to say their names and one memorable tidbit about themselves (e.g., "I'm Alicia and I love Twizzlers." Or "I'm John and I love jumping out of airplanes."). She then watches the video over the next few days to get the names and the facts memorized. Sending the videos to the class can help students memorize one another's names too. It's important that students learn each other's names as well to build class cohesion.

DISCUSSION MANAGEMENT

The Influence of Classroom Climate and Teacher Ethos

One of the most frequent complaints we hear from colleagues is that students disrespect each other during class discussion and need to be "managed" as people. We know that interaction needs to be organized and conducted in a respectful manner. There are three things a teacher can do to manage class discussion:

- First, set up a positive communication climate that is conducive to effective communication.
- Second, facilitate discussion using a procedure of fairness and effectiveness.
- Third, use discussion rules to minimize or eliminate racism, sexism, and other biased or inappropriate interaction.

Let's look at each of these issues in more detail. (We will explore discussion as an instructional strategy in Chapter 4.)

Ever since Jack Gibb published his now-famous essay on defensive communication in 1961 (see Chapter 7) in the *Journal of Communication*, we have been aware of the fundamental characteristics of a supportive (positive) communication climate that facilitate effective group interaction. Using a series of pairs, Gibb demonstrated how people achieved better interaction if their communication was descriptive, problem-oriented, spontaneous, empathic, equality-oriented, and provisional rather than evaluative, control-oriented, strategic, neutral, superior, and certain. Many teachers of interpersonal communication use Gibb's pairs to teach about the communication climate within a dyad, so why not apply it to classroom climate as well? After all, the teacher's job is to teach and model interpersonal skills. We try very hard to model empathy even when a student is describing an opinion or life experience that we don't agree with or we think may be trivial. You have to remember that if you invite students to give examples or share life experiences, you need to be ready for both immature and mature responses. If someone perceives you to be an empathic person, it will help that person to disclose appropriately, thus facilitating the learning process in an interpersonal communication course.

We find that a happy class is one where students are laughing, the teacher tells good jokes or can play off the humor set up in class, and people are just having fun as they learn. It turns out that research backs up the effectiveness of humor. Communication professors Melissa Wanzer and Ann Frymier (1999) found that teachers with a high humor orientation have a positive correlation with students' perceptions of learning; yet, that humor must be deemed appropriate by students (Wanzer, Frymier, Wojtaszczyk, & Smith, 2006). When students tell us that they *love* interpersonal communication and that they use what they learn in class all the time in their everyday lives, it tells us the class material is relevant, but it also tells us the students return day after day because they like coming to class. They *are* having fun. Something good is happening there, and part of that is the safe space that encourages positive and open communication.

One of the biggest dimensions of a positive communication climate is your own ethos (e.g., trustworthiness, competence, goodwill) as a teacher. Students develop a liking for you because of the ethos you project as a teacher and a person. Such liking then translates into student perceptions of learning, course value, and positive ratings of instruction (Comstock, Rowell, & Bowers, 1995; Moore, Masterson, Christophel, & Shea, 1996; Thweatt & McCroskey, 1998). Professors with high ethos are very much like the Aristotelian model of moral character (Kennedy, 1991), embodied in speaker language and action. In contemporary research, teacher credibility has been translated into Albert Mehrabian's (1971) concept of immediacy. Mehrabian's work suggests that teachers can develop rapport with their students through the use of nonverbal communication such as animated gestures, smiling with talking, a relaxed posture, and significant eye contact with all students in the class. Alicia trains her teaching assistants to move from behind the computer desk when using PowerPoint so that students feel more connected to them. Mehrabian's research also suggests that teachers can create greater immediacy through verbal strategies such as asking students how they feel about topics, engaging in small talk with students before and after class, and using students' names throughout discussions. Students respond to your ethos as motivation for their own work productivity.

An instructor who projects ethos to students is Mark Orbe of Western Michigan University. He attracts students through his enthusiasm, knowledge, pleasant affect, respect for others, and inviting ways of teaching. He typifies the ethos of what is expected in an interpersonal communicator, and students respond to that. His use of the African concept *dumela* (see Chapter 1) is a central component of his ethos because it embodies his own co-cultural theory (Orbe, 1998; Orbe & Bruess, 2005). *Dumela* is connected to the idea of affirming others based on interpersonal standpoints and simultaneously creating community. As a guest lecturer in Elizabeth's class, he managed to create a positive communication climate through his own ethos within five minutes of walking into the room. The way he called out "dumela" to begin the class and then praised student comments energized the students and had them paying close attention. He is a role model for us all.

Student standpoint — that is, the sum of demographics, personality, and life experience — is something we cannot control. You do not know who the thirty-five people will be coming through the door and whether or not they will jell as a group. Generally, the group either jells within the first week or it doesn't. If the group jells (and it really is a mysterious dynamic), then the class members will relate well to each other throughout the semester. If the group doesn't jell, it's a disaster. Elizabeth had this experience with a writing-intensive version of her interpersonal course. The majority of the students were nonmajors and had one goal: to get the W credit on the transcript. From the first day, there was no

---

FROM THE CLASSROOM: Setting the Tone

There is one thing that contributes to creating a positive climate from the first day of class that lasts throughout the semester. The instructor has to be sincerely excited about teaching and model excellent interpersonal communication skills. Students respect a good listener who exhibits a sense of fair-mindedness, respect, openness, and a collaborative spirit.

Marion Boyer
Instructor
Kalamazoo Valley Community College

_____

SOURCE: Personal correspondence with Elizabeth Natalle, April 26, 2006.

---

genuine concern for the course or for other students in the class. She picked up on the negative aura right away and asked if students would prefer a different seating arrangement. They chose a circle, but not everyone was happy with that. Many students sat silently and looked at the floor. When she put them in groups, they did better. Yet when it came time to role-play and volunteer for an in-class activity, no one wanted to participate. By the third class period, she said to the class that they were in this together and needed some energy. Few students responded. This class caused Elizabeth to lose sleep! What was wrong? Over the course of the semester, she tried every instructional strategy she could think of to draw them out. After poor grades on the first exam, she asked students to write a one-paragraph response on the back of the exam about their performance. The most frequent comment was: "This class is not in my major, so I just didn't spend much time studying for the exam." A couple of communication majors emerged as the regular contributors (no surprise there), but the rest of the class just didn't seem to care. It was everything she could do to stay positive and try to keep the class going. In the end, she finally came to the conclusion that this was a class composition that didn't work. It never jelled. Elizabeth was disappointed, but she had done her best to deliver a good class. The next semester, one of the students from that class enrolled in two more of her classes. When she saw him on the first day, she laughed and said, "Hey, you want to try another Natalle class after last semester?" He laughed too and said, "You know, that was the weirdest group of people I have ever been in class with. They just didn't want to be together." This same student clicked off interpersonal vocabulary and concepts right and left as they applied to the gender class we were in, so Elizabeth knew he learned in spite of the strange configuration of classmates. These things happen. Do your best, and try not to lose too much sleep.

Facilitating Discussion

In *The Argument Culture* (1998), author Deborah Tannen opens with this premise: "This book is about a pervasive warlike atmosphere that makes us approach public dialogue, and just about anything we need to accomplish, as if it were a fight" (p. 3). She explores the idea that Americans are taught to be adversarial and seem to prefer debate over dialogue. In school we learn how to criticize and find loopholes, and by the time we are graduate students we engage in the deconstruction of every idea presented to us. Tannen encourages readers to rethink debate as a general communication approach and to learn the rules of engagement for dialogue as a more effective tool for building relationships. She invokes Amitai Etzioni's *The New Golden Rule* (1996) as a helpful source of rules for being an effective dialogic partner. We agree with both Tannen and Etzioni that exploring ideas and building a spirit of inquiry might be more useful than debating a correct answer, especially when it comes to interpersonal issues where there are different standpoints. To that end, good teachers need to have a degree of expertise in facilitation skills. Leading good discussions is an artful skill, and one that takes much practice to develop.

Education majors do receive training in facilitating discussion, but most communication majors are assumed to be effective in all kinds of talk. This just isn't true. Our interpersonal texts include chapters on conversation management in dyads (e.g., DeVito, 2004; Verderber & Verderber, 2004), but why not go beyond that and train teaching assistants to manage discussion in the classroom? Although *conversation* and *discussion* are similar in that they both have a beginning, a middle, and an end and include turn-taking, they are also distinct. Conversations, according to Verderber and Verderber (2004), "are locally managed sequential interchanges of thoughts and feelings between two or more people that are interactive and largely extemporaneous" (pp. 150–151). In contrast, "discussion occurs when a group of persons assemble in a face-to-face [or computer-mediated] situation and through oral [or written] interaction exchange information or attempt to reach a decision on shared problems" (Gulley, 1968, p. 5). Note that *dialogue* (Bohm, 2004) is even something different from conversation and discussion because dialogue is technically seen as deep, empathic communication in which partners with profound differences are trying to come to an understanding. This is not usually the type of communication found in introductory interpersonal communication courses, even though the word *dialogue* is used frequently but incorrectly to refer to classroom discussion.

Students in an interpersonal communication class often mistakenly think that discussion is conversation. One of the biggest challenges is dealing with a constant revelation of personal experience that is trivial, not related to the concept at hand, and repetitive. References to talk shows and reality TV abound. The "me too" syndrome is always at work in an interpersonal classroom — students want to share with each other that their lives are the same. Elizabeth once had a Russian postdoctoral fellow who, after the first week of attending class, observed, "You know, American students like to hear themselves talk. They say anything, whether it's relevant or not. It's all about their personal experience. As much as I appreciate that freedom, why aren't they more interested in the concepts?" That wasn't the first time we've heard that type of criticism about American students, but hearing it about her own students woke Elizabeth up to the fact that she could do a better job managing discussion. It isn't easy getting students to realize that social conversation and discussion achieve different goals. The latter is an instructional strategy that is characterized by the teacher's ability to facilitate the communication toward the learning goal.

Good facilitation skills are characterized by artful control. The teacher is guiding the class toward understanding while giving participants the opportunity to contribute to that exploration of the concept. The discussion needs to have

- an introduction of the concept;
- a call for contributions that involve possible ways of understanding the concept;
- links from discussion comments to the research base behind the concept (linking theory and practice); and
- closure on what was learned through discussion.

Recording key ideas or talking points on the board may be a running activity throughout the discussion, and students would be expected to take notes (something they may need to be reminded to do since notetaking does not occur to all students as an automatic activity). Writing your students' comments on the board shows that their ideas "count," validates their contributions, and encourages them to participate further.

From a procedural point of view, the discussion leader needs to

- move the progression of the discussion forward within the time limit allowed;
- give people an opportunity to speak;
- diplomatically cut off people who want to talk too much;
- draw out people whose faces indicate they want to comment even when their hands aren't raised;
- ask questions that probe;
- synthesize comments or point out differences; and
- summarize, come to closure, and transition to the next part of the class.

Facilitating while standing up is most beneficial to us because it allows us to see everyone in the room. We can move around the room taking the energy to the person speaking at the moment, we can run to the board and jot down ideas (unless a student is doing that for the class), and our movement keeps everyone involved. However, if sitting gets the job done, do what is comfortable for you. Don't forget to take notes on what you wrote on the board before you erase it.

If the discussion centers on relational dialectics, for example, then the teacher needs to have knowledge of, at the very least, the textbook. The discussion leader has to anticipate the questions that will arise from discussions that can extend beyond the textbook. The teacher needs to have read the key work on relational dialectics, including Leslie Baxter and Barbara Montgomery's *Relating* (1996) and William Rawlins's *Friendship Matters* (1992). The teacher needs to be prepared to discuss the dialectical tensions in relationships, how those tensions manifest themselves in relational life, and how communication assists in the negotiation of dialectical tension. This knowledge is in addition to general facilitation skills! Every time you lead discussion, you bring your knowledge to bear on the discussion process itself. The deeper your knowledge, the better the discussion.

Online discussions often occur through course management systems, discussion lists, or bulletin board systems. We will discuss online discussions more in Chapter 6 on computer-mediated communication.

Rules for Discussion

The last discussion management technique to use is a kind of rule system that promotes smooth process and enhances the quality of discussion content. Students (and sometimes teachers) can be dominant and try to do all the talking. Even worse are people who exhibit rude or disrespectful treatment of others. If you use a rule system, it can be presented on the first day of class and included in the syllabus, or the class can make the rules and the instructor can distribute them later.

What would a printed set of rules look like? Following is a sample set that could serve as a model if you want to compose your own for more effective classroom discussion. This sample comes from a set of rules Elizabeth composed to help first-semester, first-year students survive a gender relationships class. The division of content and process guidelines will help a less-experienced student see that effective discussion considers both types of rules. We present this set of rules as it might appear on a classroom handout.

Computer-mediated discussion also requires its own set of guidelines. We'll discuss these rules further in Chapter 6 on computer-mediated communication.

Tolerance and Diversity of Views

So far we have discussed the ideas of how communication climate, including teacher ethos, influences student willingness to engage in discussion; procedures for facilitating discussions; and rules for the engagement of process and content in discussion. In today's classroom, discussion takes place among students who hold different political and social views that can create problems of racism, sexism, homophobia, ageism, and other forms of intolerance.

Students with little or no knowledge of difference often find it difficult to discuss diversity issues, especially when they are asked to consider thinking about and perceiving the world in ways other than what they are familiar with; their sense of knowledge and safety becomes threatened. This is especially true of first-generation college students who may have limited experience outside their own small communities and have grown up with more people similar to themselves than different. Even a decade ago, our textbooks did not really consider diversity issues very well. It was up to the teacher to try and bring these issues to the class and moderate the heated discussion that usually ensued. Today our textbooks do discuss racist, sexist, and heterosexist language (see, e.g., DeVito, 2011). Cultural considerations and viewpoints of all types — from Caucasian to African American, from male to female, from gay to straight — not only

CST 207 INTERPERSONAL COMMUNICATION: How to Engage in Class Discussion

Classroom discussions require a different kind of speech from what you might use when talking with friends. To get the most out of discussion as a learning tool, the following guidelines will assist you in your communication choices.

Content Guidelines

1. Class discussions are generally not open forums. Rather, they have the purpose of serving as a learning tool. Through group conversation, participants learn more about required reading assignments and the way theoretical matter connects to students' lives. So come to discussion prepared! Complete the reading and have questions or reactions to the material that might serve as helpful discussion.
2. Think about the content of discussion and the flow of ideas so you can make a meaningful contribution. Add ideas that extend what is being talked about, or offer your perspective as a way to clarify the issues. If you disagree with what's being advocated, back up your reasons for disagreeing with material from the reading assignments.
3. Let the facilitator (usually the professor) keep the group moving forward in its ideas and themes, but don't be afraid to ask questions or make connections from previous class discussions.
4. Stay away from thoughtless comments that are sexist or racist or demean a speaker because of his or her background or beliefs. Think before you speak, and develop a tolerance for diversity!

Process Guidelines

1. Take turns and be respectful of others when they have the floor. Only one person at a time can be heard.
2. Listen when others are speaking. Engaging in conversation with your neighbor means you can't hear the speaker. Then you will get confused and eventually lost. As you listen, evaluate the ideas of the speaker so you can react thoughtfully.
3. Take notes to keep up with your own and others' ideas. This may help you come back to an important point later and make a valuable contribution.
4. Do not shout each other down. Respectful tone of voice is expected.
5. Do not curse or use slang terms that border on distasteful or disrespectful. There simply is no place in the classroom for this type of vocabulary.
6. Assume we are all doing our best to understand material and make contributions.
7. Everyone should speak in a discussion. Give quiet people a chance to say something by not dominating the floor.
8. Stay alert and open-minded to ideas. This is a great way to learn something new!

regularly appear now (see, e.g., McCornack, 2013), but they all have credibility in the classroom as well. In spite of this progress, however, many students still find it uncomfortable talking about these topics or recognizing the validity of others' viewpoints. Indeed, it is a challenging time to be caught in the so-called culture wars (Rosen, 2003), especially in the interpersonal communication classroom. Hence, it is important to conscientiously include a tolerance policy in the list of general discussion rules. The expectation of tolerance should be explicitly expressed for students — see, for example, Content Rule #4 presented in the box on page 52.

Tolerating diverse viewpoints is as much about power as it is about what ideas may be in control in a classroom and how we respect others as human beings. Lynn Weber Cannon, sociologist and professor of women's studies at Memphis State University, was the expert who tuned us in to the assumptions, goals, and outcomes of meeting diversity in the college classroom. In a workshop Elizabeth took with Professor Cannon in 1989, she learned some valuable ideas about how to approach the concept of diversity, and we use this information to facilitate discussion and enforce rules. Here are condensed notes from that workshop. This information is for you, the teacher, to keep in mind.

THE ASSUMPTIONS BEHIND MEETING DIVERSITY IN THE CLASSROOM

- The teacher-student relationship is a social relation in which power is vested in teachers by virtue of their middle-class position in the social structure.
- In small group settings such as classrooms, powerless people are less likely to talk, have their ideas validated, and be perceived as making significant contributions to group tasks.
- Material about race, class, gender, and so forth is emotionally charged, as well as intellectually challenging.
- People want to learn about each other (despite their fears).

GOALS AND OUTCOMES OF MEETING DIVERSITY IN THE CLASSROOM

The broadest goal of the course is to empower students and

- to promote understanding and an open appreciation of diversity in American life.
- to treat every student as a unique human being, to appreciate every one of them, and to treat them equally (but certainly not the same).
- to develop a classroom environment in which the traditional racism, sexism, and classism in the university and in society are not replicated.
- to enhance the expression of diversity among students in the work they do.
- to deal with a wide range of authentic feelings among learners: discomfort, frustration, excitement, and satisfaction.

When promoting tolerance in the classroom, we also need to incorporate it into our teaching approach to facilitate good discussion and to explore our students' range of experiences in dealing with diversity issues. Each summer Alicia co-teaches a week-long special topics interpersonal communication class with colleague Renee Fussell on Interracial Communication. The purpose of the class is to try to help decrease the polarization between whites and people of color by promoting a better understanding of, and sensitivity to, what is involved in interracial interactions. This one-week, 45-hour course offers an intensely immersive experience for undergraduate students. The challenge of teaching the course is managing the dialectical tension between exposing prejudices while still protecting the feelings of all students in the class. Alicia describes the class as a roller coaster. The week typically starts with a lot of ice-breakers and friendly discussion to get students comfortable with one another, and then progresses to difficult conversations about stereotypes, historical perspective on racism, and the ways in which our culture still maintains racism. Yet, by the end of the week, many of the barriers have been broken and students have become enlightened and appreciative of the diversity around them. This is all accomplished by carefully managing discussions and encouraging honesty, respect, and empathy.

General Techniques for Classroom Management

We suggest you use a range of communication techniques in class to meet the many student opinions and to encourage respectfulness in discussion of delicate matters. We both make it clear to our students that we are not trained counselors and will not entertain personal dilemmas as class discussion. We state plainly that self-disclosure should be something that would not embarrass the individual making the disclosure. We do not self-disclose too much in class as a purposeful strategy to keep the focus on the concepts as they relate to the lives of the students and to model *appropriate* disclosure as an interpersonal skill. For example, neither one of us would disclose personal information about our husbands or walk into class and reveal the content of a conflict over a personal issue. Knowing too much about the teacher can lead to gossip, which may not be healthy for the department as a whole. It's not about you, it's about the students. Research in communication and social psychology (see, e.g., Cayanus, 2004; Goldstein & Benassi, 1994; Wambach & Brothen, 1997) supports the idea that teacher self-disclosure needs to be appropriate (not too much or too little) as an instructional strategy to promote student participation and positive regard for the teacher. Jacob Cayanus of West Virginia University (2004) recommends the following:

- use positive self-disclosure rather than reveal negative assessments of yourself;
- ensure that the disclosure is relevant to the course material;
- vary the topics of disclosure;
- vary the timing on disclosure; and
- use an appropriate amount of self-disclosure.

If you model such rules for self-disclosure, students likely will follow.

Using humor often works in the classroom, and when students start breaking rules in both discussion and general responsibility, you can say things like,

"Okay, everybody, we are falling off the wagon here with our [fill in the blank with the behavior]" (personal disclosure, getting to class on time, etc.). These friendly reminders help bring students back in line as a group. If students curse or start talking about their sex lives, you can bring them back with statements like "No cursing. Come on, we are communication students," or "Let's not go there. That's too much for me to handle." All of this works well if you are firm, consistent, and nice about it.

The big problems are the mean comments from one student to another, or the dominating students who need your attention outside of class. With over forty-five years of combined teaching experience, we are both known as no-nonsense teachers. We are direct and not afraid to shut down a person who is genuinely challenging us or his or her peers for control of the class. We have both had aggressive students drop our classes after the first day or two, when they realized they would not be the one in charge. At the same time, we've had students who would not stop talking to the point that we've had to call them in our office or write them a note. These students tend to get angry and have a great deal of difficulty finding a balance of how much to contribute. A few follow-up conversations pointing out when they are contributing well and when they are not is usually enough to guide them moving forward. Alicia even takes a similar stand in e-mail communication with her students. If students send rude e-mails (e.g., sarcastic tone, lack of general politeness, missing salutations, demanding tone, etc.), she gives them a quick little lesson about appropriate professional e-mails because she believes it is her job to ensure competent inter-personal communication in all contexts.

When a student gets out of control (for example, yelling in class about a grade or work responsibilities with group projects), you should let the student cool down and see if he or she will come to your office to talk things over. If there is no follow-up, encourage the student to come see you during office hours. Always start by recognizing something positive about your teacher-student relationship and say, for example, "We are both good people. I don't know what happened yesterday in class, but let's try to talk so we can under-stand and then decide what to do." At the end of the discussion, shake the stu-dent's hand and say, "I'm glad we talked. Let's do our best from now on." This will help you to get back on track and assure that the rules will be followed. But keep in mind that you need to ensure a safe conversation for you and the student. Alicia always reminds her teaching assistants to leave the office door open when talking with volatile students (even better, have another TA in the office or close by and alert others of the situation in advance). Be sure to take some notes of this experience for your records. And don't be afraid to speak to your course director, department chair, or Dean of Students about the behavior, because these sources need to know about these types of challenges and they may have some great suggestions. Keep in mind too that while conservations with challenging students might be a bit daunting for you, they are absolutely necessary, because the other students in your classroom will appreciate it as well. It is your job as the instructor to protect all of your students and ensure they feel like they can learn in a comfortable environment.

Course Policies as General Classroom Rules

In reviewing the course syllabi of other interpersonal communication instructors, we see that many professors embed or spell out general classroom rules of student responsibility. Attendance policies, for example, are rules that dictate the consequences of lateness to or absence from class. Turning in homework late, missing exams, and not completing course requirements usually carry rule-bound penalties. The university honor code is a set of rules for ethical student behavior. All of these rules help the teacher manage people and course activities so work is completed on time and the learning process can progress within the time allotted for the course. What happens when students break the rules? The teacher's responsibility is to enforce the rules, ensuring fairness to all students, and to maintain the integrity of the course. Over the years we have had many students earn grades that do not reflect their intellectual capabilities because they could not work within the rule system. As much as we hate to see grades drop over penalties, it truly is not fair to other students who do come to class and complete work on time. Stick to your rules, knowing that students will need to abide by work policies once they get into the working world.

If only the rule systems worked so smoothly in every class! That is not the case, however, when we begin to consider our students as individuals with complex lives. Most student dilemmas arise from issues outside the classroom. As professors, one thing we could all do better is to try and understand our students as, for example, first-year students away from home for the first time, or adult students with jobs and families, or perhaps students who struggle with depression. In the next section we will confront common student challenges and consider some effective responses.

STUDENT MANAGEMENT

We used to worry most over fair grading and the occasional cheater. Every once in a while a more troubling personal and serious problem, such as alcohol abuse or a violent dating partner, would arise. Now we worry about a whole generation of students who often seem less prepared for adult social interaction and behave inappropriately in the college classroom. We joke with colleagues about which will drive us to retirement first: the workload or the bizarre student behavior. Maybe media-effects theorist George Gerbner (1990) was right in his observation that the media violence that surrounds us has cultivated a "mean world syndrome" that begets more aggressive people. This has certainly trickled down to the classroom, and student dilemmas take up more time than we wish to spend on problem solving. On a regular basis we confront everything from students cursing or bullying each other in class to students talking back to us to students expecting that their personal problems excuse them from work deadlines. On rare occasions students have threatened one of us to the point that we have feared for our personal safety. Clearly there's a lot we need to be prepared for as classroom teachers, and particularly as teachers of interpersonal communication, because it is in an interpersonal classroom that such dilemmas are likely to be self-disclosed or come to public attention.

Difficult or Disruptive Students

We have been reading about and researching the phenomenon of "difficult people" since family therapist Virginia Satir published *peoplemaking* in 1971 (see Chapter 7). Interpersonal trainer Robert Lucas (2005) offers 176 tips for difficult classroom situations, including such topics as people who speak English as a second language right along with the more expected categories of difficulty: clowns, experts, agitators, monopolizers, poor listeners, and latecomers, among many others. To give advice on every type of problem student you will encounter is almost impossible because people act out in many different ways, depending on the situation. Classroom management techniques actually curb a lot of disruption because rules and a positive communication climate keep most people in order. The following three practices go a long way toward preventing difficult behavior:

1. knowing people's names and something about them, which helps to acknowledge them as people (some students simply crave confirmation);
2. inviting students to take advantage of office hours; and
3. being firm when correcting a student.

These techniques also prepare you to handle difficulties that arise unexpectedly.

Elizabeth can recall a student who was a real fan of hers in the first class they had together, but in the next class, she became a completely difficult person and started disrupting by wearing sunglasses, refusing to speak in group activities, and either handing in incomplete work or missing deadlines altogether. In class, Elizabeth politely but firmly asked her to remove the sunglasses so they could see each other. She encouraged her to make contributions to her group (because she really was bright and had much to offer). Her disruptions continued throughout the semester, and Elizabeth asked her to visit her in her office. She confronted the student and said, "Something is wrong. You are not the same person this semester and it is affecting your work and your relationships with others. Can I help?" She said simply, "I'm going through a lot." Elizabeth couldn't get any more out of her, and the student remained defiant and distant in class. Her research supervisor said the same was happening with their work together. As faculty, we remained open and offered assistance. She finished the semester with poor grades, but graduated. The faculty were sorry they couldn't do any more to help. Although the class suffered some because of her disruptive behavior, no one blamed Elizabeth or themselves, since they all had tried to bring her around. As a class they learned that patience and tolerance are part of a response, but that enforcing the rules and moving ahead also need to happen for the good of all. You will have to deal directly with difficult students, because if you don't, other students will resent it and judge you negatively on teaching evaluations for losing control of the class. Reading books is a starting point for dealing with difficult people, but we suggest you confer with your peers as well. Faculty can compare observations and take collective action as an effective way to help a student in difficulty.

Ethical Considerations and Problem Students

Ethical communication is speech that is honest, morally intact, and aimed at honoring the relationship and its goals. Many questions arise about the ethics of communication in the classroom on a daily basis. For example, is it ethical to shut down someone in class discussion for dominating? Here the issue is more a separation of the behavior from the person. What you want to curb is the domination, not the self-worth of the person. It is certainly ethical to not call on someone who always has a hand up or to say, "Let's hear from some quiet people today," as you are trying to facilitate turn-taking. There may even come a point when you have to pull a student aside and ask him or her to simply control the behavior in question. Be aware that students can get angry and bad behavior can escalate. Keep notes on problem students because you may need to solve bigger issues later. Note the box below from my own Dean of Students about bad behavior in general.

FROM THE CLASSROOM: The Most Common Interpersonal Communication Problem between Professor and Student

Having different perceptions of appropriate classroom behavior is the most common interpersonal problem between professors and students. Unclear expectations are definitely an issue. Faculty need to be clear about their expectations and consequences for not abiding by the guidelines when they are covering their syllabus during the first few class sessions. The faculty most successful at working with difficult students recommend spending the first day of class discussing what type of learning environment will be established for the class and get buy-in from students by providing an opportunity for students to contribute to the discussion of a good classroom environment. In addition, they address problem behavior immediately directly with the student and document the conversation. That way, if the behavior escalates, action can be taken immediately. At UNCG, the Disruptive Behavior in the Classroom Policy might be invoked. Oftentimes, the initial conversation with the student might yield information about personal issues that are influencing the disruptive behavior, which allows the faculty member to refer the student to an office like ours that can work with getting the student assistance.

Jen Day Shaw
Dean of Students
University of North Carolina at Greensboro

SOURCE: Personal correspondence with Elizabeth Natalle, April 25, 2006.

Similar problems arise regarding student communication to professors through e-mail. Beyond acceptable-use policies, students now engage in a variety of Internet behaviors that could be considered unethical. Journalist Jonathan Glater (2006) hit the nail on the head in a *New York Times* article that described everything from flaming a professor to demanding information or attention to criticizing the course and peers to general immaturity in requests. When students write us threatening or bizarre e-mail messages, we retain a copy of the message and report it to our department head. On one occasion, Elizabeth discovered during a faculty meeting that one student had threatened several members of faculty in different classes, so the Dean of Students was made aware of the situation. She wrote to the student and said that e-mail seemed to be a source of misunderstanding rather than clarity and that she should come to her office to communicate about assignments. She never came to Elizabeth's office but she did complete her work, and that was the end of the problem. Such situations are very uncomfortable, and we do worry about them. You may wonder if the student will escalate the verbal aggression into physical violence.

Your institution's Division of Student Affairs likely offers information that can guide you through dealing with students in distress. A pamphlet from UNC Greensboro, for example, is very helpful and contains a list of indicators (academic, emotional, physical, and safety risk) to look for if you suspect a student is having difficulty. There is also a list of ways to help, including the following points:

- Take these signs seriously.
- Meet privately with a student in distress.
- Specifically point out signs you've observed.
- Listen to the student's response.
- Refer.
- Follow university procedures.
- Recognize an urgent situation.
- Set expectations.
- Respect confidentiality.

Finally, the brochure has a list of relevant offices, contact names, and phone numbers. Find out whether your institution has such a brochure. Keep a copy with your other important resources. Always remember that if you are not a certified counselor, you must refer any troubled student to an expert. You may not legally dispense advice. The university attorney and Dean of Students are there to help, so enlist their aid as appropriate.

We want to turn now to two different types of students who may challenge you in creative ways rather than through the type of difficulty just discussed. The nontraditional or adult student is part of a growing population across the country. Such students are, indeed, different from the more traditional 18- to 24-year-olds. The other type of student you may face is the one who comes from a different cultural background, someone we might refer to as *co-cultural*. For example, if you are a Caucasian, heterosexual man, a co-cultural student in your class might be an African American lesbian. Not only will you have to negotiate those different standpoints in your teacher-student relationship, you may have to mediate between and among co-cultural students as they interact and disagree on their opinions of topics under study.

Nontraditional or Adult Students

According to researcher Marian Houser (2004), age usually is the defining characteristic of an adult learner. Many adult learners return to school after already having a family or holding years of experience in the working world. This life experience is perhaps the biggest difference between nontraditional and traditional students. Unlike traditional students, most adult learners will likely consider themselves a parent, or a working adult first, and a student second. It is important for instructors to understand and acknowledge that the different life roles adult learners play may put extra pressure on their academic success.

There can be certain challenges to teaching adult students, and your experience may vary based on the type of institution where you teach. For example, community colleges as a general pattern have more adult students enrolled than do four-year colleges in undergraduate courses. Right from the start, nontraditional students recognize their unique presence in the class simply by the way they look and dress. They might not be in the same social circles as the traditional students as well due to the demands in their personal lives and their age difference. It's important to note that nontraditional students are probably nervous about the ways they are different from their more traditional classmates. In our classrooms, if there is an adult student in the class (and there is usually only one or two), we have found that a woman will more likely make herself known than will a man. That student will talk more, be perceived by younger students as a "mom," will be more stressed over earning an A, will spend more time in our office asking about assignments, will dominate class activities by taking on self-appointed leadership roles, and will get less out of the class because she has disproportionate life experience to the material being taught. While younger students are learning to put vocabulary on life experience and looking ahead to the future, adult students — particularly parents — are more likely reflecting on past experiences. This generational difference can cause some conflict, but it is manageable, and each group can actually learn from the other.

Occasionally, adult students who are also parents may miss class when their child is sick or when there are activities at their child's school that require the parents' attendance. These students may wish to be excused when family matters take them away from class. Also, these students may make a special request more often to e-mail assignments rather than turn them in at the requested time or in class. To avoid setting up double standards that traditional college students may potentially resent, we try to be fair under the circumstances and often work with adult students on a one-on-one basis to negotiate school requirements, given the reality of family life. We have observed that many adult students will put a lot of pressure on themselves to succeed at the same time that they express a lack of confidence in their academic ability because they've been out of school for so long.

Teaching a class comprising both traditional and adult students can be quite challenging. You have to keep in mind the examples that you use in class as well as your technological requirements. Even something as simple as choosing a video clip from YouTube to share during a lecture can be challenging when you have students in different age groups with varying interests (e.g., your younger students might not remember *Seinfeld* or your older students might be unfamiliar with Snapfish). At other times having adult students and traditional students puts you in the position of mediator: You find yourself having to remind people to be respectful of each other. You have to reassure adults that they can succeed (even when they make the top grades in class), and that even though their enthusiasm is wonderful, they should not get carried away with contributions to class discussion. Although we have to be humane in recognizing that adult students *do* have different needs and face challenges that require some flexibility, we are also responsible for holding adult students accountable to general class rules. We try to capitalize on the interpersonal experiences of adult students as evidence that theories and concepts presented in the text and in class are leading us somewhere. Remember to respect the life experiences they have had and realize they can actually be an asset to class discussions through the depth and breadth they bring to the table. Marian Houser writes in an article in *Communication Teacher* (2004) that nontraditional students do have different needs and suggests the following effective strategy: "Create a positive learning environment and a non-threatening communication climate where adults feel as if they are part of the learning community. Some ways to do this are to have students interview each other, break students into groups, encourage support networking, and get to know students yourself" (p. 80). These are good suggestions and should help you mix students together for effective learning.

If you are a younger instructor, it's quite possible you may feel intimidated teaching nontraditional students because of the age difference. Some teaching assistants are afraid they won't have the appropriate knowledge base and experience they need to teach students older than they are. But it is important to remember that students and teachers can learn from each other. Teaching assistants occasionally report that adult students appear to talk down to them or show disrespect. One colleague, who is in her mid-twenties, recounted an older student who talked to the point of dominance, stayed after class every session, and then started interrupting her in lecture to "teach" the class himself. When he received a C on the first major assignment, he confronted her. She explained the grading rubric to him and outlined some suggestions for improvement. After the confrontation, he stopped staying late and interrupting lectures, but she did have to keep working on the dominance problem. The relationship between teacher and nontraditional student works best if it is based on mutual respect.

Co-cultural Student Populations

Today's diverse college classroom comprises many students from a variety of backgrounds. Mark Orbe's (1998) concept of co-cultural communication recognizes that two people from different cultural standpoints will come together and experience automatic power imbalances and a struggle for dominance based on the differences in standpoints. Think back to the example of the Caucasian, heterosexual, male teacher and the African American lesbian student — note that the two partners in this interpersonal relationship are quite different. How do you negotiate the differences in this relationship to ensure that learning is mutual? It takes a diverse number of communication strategies and cultural knowledge to achieve this negotiation. Orbe describes twenty-six different co-cultural strategies. They are worth studying to help familiarize yourself with what your students do and with what you might be doing to communicate with students who are culturally different from you.

Our own experiences have forced us more than once to negotiate our positions as Caucasian women in a variety of co-cultural relationships. In each case we had to use our knowledge, experience, or outside resources to figure out communication strategies that would help us cross a cultural gap rather than have a relational breakdown. For example, Elizabeth taught a Japanese exchange student who failed every exam and wrote e-mails apologizing for being "so stupid," even though she needed to pass the class to enroll the following semester. With only a reading knowledge of Japan, she sought out a Japanese colleague to advise her on the teacher-student relationship in Japan so that she could approach the student without scaring her. There are many types of co-cultural interactions that include people one wouldn't ordinarily think of as differing in their status or level of power. Even first-generation college students come to school without the same knowledge as students of college-educated parents (Orbe, 2004). Those students may feel powerless and uninformed, yet they need to be assimilated into the education system so they are successful. At Southern Illinois University Edwardsville where Alicia teaches, they offer "Safe Zone" training in order to help faculty learn how to interact with students from Lesbian, Gay, Bisexual, and Transgender (LGBT) communities. The Safe Zone is a network of teachers, students, and staff that are trained and committed to providing understanding and support to LGBT people who need help, advice, or just someone to listen to their struggles. The goal of the group is to encourage tolerance and to end heterosexist and homophobic words and actions through education and enlightenment. You may find organizations such as Safe Zone at your campus that could provide excellent resources for better understanding and supporting the diversity of your students.

Consider any resources you may have on campus, such as a multicultural resource center or an office for African American student affairs, for example, where you can get training, tap into resources, or seek advice in your quest to communicate effectively.

As instructors, we need to stay alert every day to the possibilities of both success and failure when cultural differences meet in the classroom. As Afrocentric theorist Molefi Asante wrote many years ago under the name Art Smith (1973), "normalization" will not occur in interracial relationships (and, by extension, co-cultural relationships) until we are willing to communicate, we make ourselves mentally and physically accessible, we appreciate that the task of communication has the potential to be difficult, and we attempt to be authentic by presenting a self that isn't masked in facade.

CONCLUSION

Student challenges will inevitably arise in an interpersonal communication course. Classroom management is an issue of controlling space, people, and discussion. It helps teachers stay organized and move forward in an orderly manner to accomplish course goals and have fun at the same time. It also helps to control student disruption and other similar behaviors. For the deeper problems, we need to remember that we are teachers, not counselors, and we need to rely on outside help when student needs go beyond the classroom. We also need to remember that we live in an ever-changing world of student demographics and standpoints. The ability to adapt to and empathize with students will help us make the most out of the classroom experience.

4

Instructional Strategies

Every introductory interpersonal communication course has inherent structural challenges that are unique to the course. In this chapter we explore five of those challenges: development of instructional strategies, balancing theory and practice, teaching the vocabulary of the discipline, use of technology, and service learning. Sorting out best practices connected to each of these areas can only strengthen the framework of your course and make your teaching more effective.

INSTRUCTIONAL STRATEGIES

An *instructional strategy* is a teaching method that facilitates learning and helps an instructor achieve course objectives. Recall from Chapter 2 that instructional strategies are one piece of the larger puzzle that is the structure of your course. There must be logical connections among the course objectives, instructional strategies, evaluation procedures, organization of course content, and syllabus. Common instructional strategies in an introductory interpersonal course include reading texts and research articles; lecturing; class, small-group, and online discussions; case-study analysis; tutorials; team teaching, in-class or laboratory activities; film viewing and analysis; fieldwork (interviewing a family member or conducting a relationship analysis); journaling; service learning; student presentations; guest speakers; and workshops. Choosing the most effective teaching style is part of the overall instructional strategy.

A new teacher may start with the primary pedagogical decision of how to balance lecturing and activities. However, developing an effective set of teaching methods is actually more complicated than that. Education professors Keith Prichard and McLaren Sawyer (1994) argue that selecting teaching methods comes down to a fairly complex set of decisions that includes at least six factors: knowledge of the research on the psychology of teaching, one's prior role models, the personality of the instructor, the teaching philosophy of the instructor, outside influences on the academy (such as the public mood on political correctness), and the teaching context (such as a small- versus a large-enrollment course). You also have to consider your departmental norms and expected outcomes as well as university expectations for your course.

Regarding the first factor, what we know about students' learning styles today is that most tend to be visual learners with short attention spans. As one reviewer of this book commented, "Every year it seems like I have to work harder and be more creative in order to keep my students interested." Another reviewer reminded me that when selecting instructional strategies, it might be helpful to consider the typological preferences (e.g., Myers-Briggs Type Indicators®) or learning styles (e.g., Kolb's learning style inventory or the VARK Questionnaire) of both the teacher and the students. For example, teachers who are strong extroverts may have to consider how best to relate to students who are more introverted when it comes to discussions.

Factor five from Prichard and Sawyer concerning outside influences relates to how the surrounding political or religious environment can affect one's teaching decisions. Elizabeth lives in the "Bible Belt" of America, so it was a big decision for her to start talking about gay and lesbian families when the text-books didn't have much on that topic in the chapter on family relationships. She initially inserted the topic in a mini-lecture that introduced the textbook chapter. She always gives a quick statistical look at the current status of the American family. Students then often nod, "yeah, that's me" when they recognize a family configuration that describes them. This sets the stage for students to talk and contribute examples of communication from a diverse range of family relationships. Most texts now include something about gay and lesbian families, which adds credibility to the topic and diffuses some of the controversy in the teaching decision.

The teaching context may include the fact that many communication courses now play a central role in "communication across the curriculum" programs. Speaking- and writing-intensive courses require a course structure and instructional strategies that help students use speaking and writing both as literacy skills and as tools for expressing their thoughts. You may have to build into the course exercises or assignments that achieve particular objectives for communication-intensive courses. At our institutions, teachers can attend workshops and receive assistance with those decisions; find out if your institution offers help as well.

Locating Instructional Strategies

New teachers will initially find instructional strategies in the textbook and the accompanying instructor's manual. For an interpersonal course, this implies two things: First, students will be expected to read chapters and then come to class and discuss them (most likely in a lecture-discussion format). Second, instructors will probably engage students in class activities that will enable them to practice or realize how a concept works. Elizabeth still does this as a successful set of instructional strategies after thirty years in the classroom. If students are buying a text, they expect to use it. Elizabeth uses the text every day as part of her delivery of instruction. She may say, "Let's look at the chart on confirming and disconfirming language in our text so we can talk about how that works in our relationships." Or, "Tonight I want you to take the love styles test in the text so we can talk about that in our next class period." Teachers can also encourage their students to use the web resources provided with their texts. Students often enjoy the text Web site because they can get additional information on the course concepts and see video examples all while sitting in the location of their choice. We use information, assessments, and text activities as part of the overall instructional strategy. Why is this good for new instructors as well as old hands? Entry-level students want the reassurance of a textbook, and reading a book is a primary way of learning in our educational system. Reading and discussing a text, followed by an in-class exercise, is probably the most common instructional strategy in an interpersonal communication course. One of Elizabeth's students, Michelle Lewis, put it well when she said, "Exercises and activities have really helped me learn the material. The role playing and skits helped the material become more of a 'real life' situation. For me, I was able to take the activities and reflect back on my relationships" (personal correspondence with Elizabeth, June 15, 2006).

In addition to the text and instructor's manual, most instructors keep files of activities and assignments they've collected over the years from observing other classes, attending convention panels or workshops where these strategies are presented (e.g., GIFTS, or great ideas for teaching speech, are common at communication conferences), culling issues of *Communication Teacher*, talking to colleagues around the country, and modifying activities from their own days as students. Instructors might also go online and get activities from Web sites, although caution is recommended.

What works among all these possible strategies? Many things do — that's for sure. You will probably engage in trial and error as you get comfortable and reflect on some of the factors outlined by Prichard and Sawyer (1994) just discussed. We can tell you that interactive strategies that involve energy, student participation, and fun are what draw students to the material. If they are having fun and learning at the same time, they will keep coming back. Professional speaker Karen Lawson (1999) states in her book *Involving Your Audience: Making It Active* that audience involvement is crucial because it establishes rapport, reinforces key points, gathers information about your audience, gains and maintains their attention, energizes the group, and provides entertainment. Indeed, these six reasons for participation are key for lectures and discussions in the classroom as well. Further, she recommends a three-step formula for success in implementing participation with audiences that we think can be useful in the classroom as well:

1. **Introduce the activity.** Be sure to clearly explain what you want your students to do during the activity. Provide background and detailed instructions in verbal and visual formats.
2. **Conduct the activity.** Be sure to use your facilitation skills to walk around and ensure your students understand the objective of your activity. Clarify instructions if necessary and be sure they are staying on track (prevent off-task chatter).
3. **Debrief the activity.** This is a very important step that is often forgotten! Many instructors move on past the activity not realizing that they are missing crucial learning moments. To ensure that your activity is not just for entertainment, be sure to process what you wanted students to gain from the activity. Help them see the parallels and meanings between

their experience in the activity, events in their own lives, and the related course concepts.

During the course of a semester our students are involved in at least eight to ten activities requiring a response on a 5 × 8 card, three to five role-plays, one case study, three to five small-group discussions, five to six charts on the board to be filled in, six to ten demonstrations or quick practices, and three to five additional scales or assessments. This is in a class that meets twice a week for sixteen weeks. There is something active going on every day in addition to lectures, discussions, and other forms of instructional delivery. As topics develop, we bring in newspaper clippings and create additional in-class activities to address breaking topics.

Getting Students to Read

Reading assigned chapters in the textbook is the most common instructional strategy employed by instructors, yet one of their biggest concerns is that students come to class without having read the assigned material from the text or the reserved reading list. We experience this problem all the time. What happens then? A punitive approach is to give quizzes or to ask students who didn't read to leave the class. More motivational approaches include asking each student to bring a 5 × 8 index card to class with a reaction to the reading or an application of a concept from his or her own life. Jump ahead to Chapter 7 and look at the section on reading resources efficiently. Material from that section could be used to compose a handout to help students better comprehend the textbook.

We also suggest that you give your students some overall reading tips, especially for freshmen who may not have had heavy reading loads in their high school courses. For example, remind your students to avoid the tendency to open to the first page of a chapter and immediately dig into the first line. Instead, encourage them to look through the entire chapter to get a grasp on the overall goals of the chapter. Having this kind of overview will help them logically place the information as they move throughout the chapter. Remind students to look at any pictures provided and look for bold concepts before they begin as well. We give these tips to our for first- and second-year students and they have proven useful.

During class you can ask students what they think of the reading. This is a consistent practice for us because we want to emphasize for students the relationship between reading and thoughtful class discussions. Students who do not read simply do not participate as well in class, nor do they perform at high levels on exams. A show of hands in our own classes reveals that anywhere from one-third to two-thirds of the students have not read on any given day. It is hard to ignore the fact that students do not read before coming to class, so we need to be proactive in confronting this reality.

English professor and writing expert John Bean demonstrates how critical thinking, writing, and reading all intersect when we teach students to solve problems actively rather than passively. In his book *Engaging Ideas* (1996), Bean advises teachers on how to help students read. In addition to the standard suggestions of showing students how to take notes in the margins of a book and prepare cards with thesis statements from the reading, he offers the following tips:

- Develop student interest in readings by discussing in advance problems or issues that may then be addressed in the reading.
- Create reading guides if the texts involve cultural codes or knowledge of difficult vocabulary and then discuss those items after the reading is done.
- Ask students to keep a "reading log" in which they make journal-like entries with ideas and responses triggered by the reading. Use those responses to launch class discussions.
- Provide one or two questions students must respond to after doing the assigned reading. Use the answers in class discussion.
- Ask students to summarize in their own words particularly difficult passages.

Note that all of these strategies could employ 5 × 8 cards that are then handed in for you to review. Other strategies that Alicia has used in her undergraduate and graduate interpersonal communication classes include one-word journals, "nugget papers," and guided free-writes. One-word journals involve having students read a chapter in advance of class or reading a passage in class and then asking each student to write one word to describe the reading. Then, students follow up with a short paragraph description for why they chose this word. The students' chosen words can be used to form a list on the chalkboard. The instructor can compare similarities and differences in the chosen words and ask students to share their rationale for their choices. For "nugget papers" students are asked to type a one-page paper before class that highlights the three to five interesting nuggets of information or "ah-ha moments" students gathered from the reading. Then, Alicia calls on students throughout the class discussion to share their nuggets. She has also added to this weekly assignment by asking students to create two discussion questions covering the reading that can be used for paired or group discussions. She also utilizes a variety of free-writes by asking students to spend one to two minutes writing about the assigned reading at the beginning of the class. Guided free-writes include having students write answers to specific discussion questions or giving them a paragraph from the reading to which to respond. By helping students to read better, there is every expectation that other aspects of learning, such as discussions and completion of assignments, will also improve.

Team Teaching

Team teaching is an instructional strategy that is well suited to an interpersonal communication course, but we do not use it often enough because of economic reasons. Instructor teams could serve as the model of an effective dyad. Note that having a teaching assistant is not necessarily team teaching, unless the TA is a true part of shared instruction for the course. One successful instructor team is Steven McCornack and Kelly Morrison, a husband-and-wife team at Michigan State University; together they teach an entry-level course that enrolls almost 650 students a semester. While we can't even imagine what it takes to be skillful enough to pull that off, they both love it. One key to success in team teaching is really knowing your co-teacher well and sharing a similar teaching philosophy. After a while, the team will grow and become a kind of synchronized whole. Here's what the MSU team has to say:

KELLY

I really enjoy team-teaching this course. It is truly beneficial to have two seasoned lecturers in there because while one is talking the other can be observing the class to gauge understanding and decide whether or not a concept needs to be explained again or clarified with an additional example. The most challenging aspects are making sure that it doesn't seem to the students that one person is more knowledgeable than another (i.e., one person is the "lead" and the other the "assistant"), especially when gender roles come into play. It is also challenging to team teach if you get in a fight right before lecture, or disagree with something they are saying or the way they are presenting an idea. (Personal correspondence with Elizabeth, June 6, 2006)

STEVE

It's great *fun* to teach with such an excellent co-instructor, with whom I share so much history. We can "play off" each other quite a bit. But it's also a challenge. Even though there are large points of agreement and "deals" struck in advance regarding how things should and will be covered, when it comes to the particulars everyone has their own unique view of things, and it's frequently the case that one or the other of us thinks, "Well, that's not *quite* how I would have explained it." Team teaching is like playing in a band. You know what your potential is, but that potential is fully realized only on certain occasions. (Personal correspondence with Elizabeth, June 1, 2006)

Alicia team teaches a one-week intensive undergraduate class on Interracial Communication every summer with colleague Renee Fussell and asserts that it is often like being in a marriage; you need a strong marital coalition to deal with the many challenges that come your way. You have to ensure that both of you are on the same page in terms of policies and assignment expectations. Sometimes students can try the old trick, "If mom says no, ask dad." That is, they can ask for special concessions from your partner right after you have already said no. To avoid this trap, try to make an agreement beforehand about how to handle such situations. You also need to make decisions in advance for how you will cover grading. Will you each take a portion of the grading? Will you both grade everything together and agree on a grade? Will you grade each project separately and create an average of the two? If team teaching is an instructional strategy you want to employ, investigate the policies and attitudes toward this unique approach. Be sure you have a compatible partner who is willing to commit to team teaching for more than one semester. It takes time to perfect this strategy.

Instruction on the First Day of Class

What impression would you like to make on the first day? How will the first day of your interpersonal communication course set the tone for the rest of the semester? The first day of class gets a lot of attention from pedagogy experts. Wilbert McKeachie's famous book, *Teaching Tips* (1969), discussed what to do on the first day, and we are still getting advice (e.g., Friedrich & Cooper, 1999) on how to overview a course and present ourselves to meet the expectations of students. Graduate assistant supervisor Katherine Hendrix (2000) even provides a helpful checklist of behaviors to perform on the first day, from identifying yourself (yes, some people forget to introduce themselves!) to staying after class for a few minutes to answer questions or greet students who wish to speak to you. If you are new to teaching, or if you just want to refresh your memory on the technical procedures of what to do, say, and bring to class, Hendrix's guide is a good source.

The first day of class is important in demonstrating to students what to expect from your instruction. In communication courses, a common first day schedule is to hand out the syllabus, conduct an icebreaker activity so students can get to know one another, and end the class early. Many instructors do not want to start any content because there are absences, adds and drops, and general jockeying for the line-up of a final roll sheet. Students are excited the first day, or lost, or hung over, and generally not expecting to do any cognitive work. We think it's a waste of time not to cover any content because, in spite of all the logistical problems just mentioned, we want to show students that we are serious, that there is *great* content in the course, and that we need to get started!

Some professors do not pass out the syllabus on the first day. If the syllabus has been posted online, the professor may direct the students to the posting and answer questions on the second day of class or through e-mail. A colleague of ours who refrains from handing out the syllabus on the first day does so because he wants to shake things up and not be predictable. For the most part, however, professors do pass out and discuss the syllabus. We do so because many students at our schools commute and work full-time. Some are trying to balance their course load and need to see a syllabus to decide if it is the right time to take this course. We certainly respect that and let the students know what to expect through a syllabus.

We spend the next portion of the class period introducing core concepts in a mini-lecture on interpersonal communication. Elizabeth likes to talk to her students about the five assumptions that point toward the key concepts underlying our study of interpersonal communication: communication is the basis of relating, empathy, understanding self and other, making communication choices, and understanding the consequences of choices. This sounds boring, but it is not. It is a fascinating, sincere, and intelligent set of ideas that sets us up for both the philosophical and the practical units in the course curriculum. The course and her efficacy as an instructor get overviewed in this way.

The last portion of class is the icebreaker. Elizabeth has a fun activity where the students pair off in dyads, get to know each other, and name a characteristic of an effective interpersonal relationship based on their knowledge and experiences. They then introduce each other to the rest of the class and we make the list of characteristics (e.g., honesty, trust, good listening). They have fun meeting one another and talking about the list as it is generated. The list, along with the initial assumptions, is then used during the next class period to launch a discussion of definitions and is further used in an exercise the following week in which students build their own models of the interpersonal communication process. In fact, the material from the first day is still referred to on the last day of class as everything comes full circle. Everything is strategic about the first day and is designed to set the pace, introduce content, establish instructor credibility, and let students introduce themselves. The classroom climate is established by the end of the class period, expectations are laid out, and we all have a good idea of whether the class is going to work. For both of us, the first day is very exciting, and we always look forward to meeting new students and persuading them to be just as enthusiastic about interpersonal communication as we are!

A note on impression management on the first day: dress for success. If you are trying to model effective communication, dressing to honor the professional nature of the classroom is appropriate. Students scrutinize every move you make and every piece of clothing you wear. Try to minimize clothing choice as something that could be negative or could bias the way students relate to you.

On the first day, wear your best smile and be your most open. Use that day to create the kind of learning community that reflects your overall philosophy of interpersonal communication. For example, Professor Bill Rawlins of Ohio University establishes a sense of community from the first day forward. Professor Rawlins is well known in interpersonal communication circles as a kind, soft-spoken, and philosophical person. He's a big believer in dialogue as the best approach to negotiating the partnership of a dyad. Rawlins creates a classroom environment around the Aristotelian notion of civic friendship. From the first day, he encourages students to be who they are (the Buberian notion of the authentic self) and to thrive on the unique insights each person will bring to the classroom. He says, in effect, "We are a political community where we grow together in the freedom to be different from each other" (personal conversation, June 12, 2006). In this community, Rawlins and his students spend the semester studying interpersonal communication in a safe environment (psychologically, emotionally) in which he asks his students to be who they are apart from all the distractions of the world around them. This is accomplished through his ability to suspend judgment and welcome all students in dialogue about the issues at hand.

BALANCING THEORY AND PRACTICE

Regardless of years of experience, instructors overwhelmingly talk about the challenge of trying to balance theory with practice in the interpersonal communication classroom. Three reasons explain why we struggle with this so much:

1. The "touchy-feely" approach to teaching in the early 1970s has left us with a bad reputation for being without content (that is, theory).
2. Students recoil at the idea of getting too involved with theory because it seems difficult.
3. Textbooks seem to emphasize skills and practice over in-depth examinations of theory.

We try to find a balance by selecting particular theories that we want to spend more time on because they are important to a student's knowledge and understanding of the interpersonal communication process. In our classes, the theories that fit this category include the following (see Chapter 7 for sources on these theories):

- social exchange/equity,
- attribution,
- uncertainty reduction,
- rules,
- negotiation of self,
- relational dialectics,
- stage theory,
- communication competence,
- gendered conversational style,
- conflict management, and
- intercultural communication theories.

Depending on the depth we go into, students receive extra information in lecture, handouts in their course packets with information and suggested readings, or reserve readings. These theories get played out in assignments and class activities, and we use them as often as possible when answering questions or engaging in discussion. Our goal is to develop critical thinking and problem-solving skills about relationships that involve a theoretical frame of reference.

Making consistent references to theory is a strategy that also demonstrates to students that an educated individual has the critical thinking skills and the appropriate communication knowledge to approach the world as a reality that needs some kind of an explanation. Theory is the tool that helps us solve problems, enjoy a higher quality of life, and understand behavior and attitudes in our relationships with others. In a short period of time, we hear students discussing theory among themselves, or they come to class telling us how they applied uncertainty reduction, for example, to a situation in their own lives. This shows us that a "mind-map" is beginning to form in their heads as a coherent way to approach real-world relationships. Above all, we approach the study of the interpersonal communication process with cognitive, behavioral, and emotional intelligence. The balance of theory and practice is the manifestation of that intelligence.

Colleagues tell us that stories and examples work best in helping students understand how to put theory into practice. Our students also report that examples are one of the best ways they learn. So for every concept we teach in class, we give an example. For example, when Alicia discusses Leslie Baxter and Barbara Montgomery's Relational Dialectics theory, she always tells the story of her wedding to explain autonomy and connection. She recalls fondly how the minister asked the bride and groom during the ceremony to light the unity candle while urging them not to blow out their individual candles. This act symbolizes the notion that joint identity is just as crucial as individual identity. To this day, students can relate to the idea of the unity candle representing the importance of connection while the individual candles represent the importance of individuality or autonomy. You can also ask your students for relevant examples—after all, they are often sitting in class thinking of them anyway and they love to share their experiences. However, keep in mind that instructor examples are often more developed and might be a more accurate representation of concepts. When asking students for examples, be ready to carefully guide the discussion so it doesn't get off track.

One caution about stories: Do not let students get the upper hand. One of Elizabeth's colleagues, Jessica Delk, expressed frustration with students telling stories from personal experience and losing sight of the theoretical idea under study. She summed it up: "I do find this tie back to theory to be problematic and not where they [the students] want to focus their energy" (personal correspondence with Elizabeth, October 4, 2004). Although we all want students to participate and share the responsibility of linking theory to real life, the teacher must control the amount of storytelling and the linkage to theory. This takes skill in facilitation and discussion leadership, as discussed in Chapter 3.

There are alternatives to stories and examples. To explore uncertainty reduction theory, Elizabeth asks students to analyze a case study in groups of four to six people for about fifteen to twenty minutes. The case accomplishes a lot more than just "practicing" theory because the content of the case involves an interracial relationship that gets students talking about cultural issues and how racism and uncertainty might be related. As an instructional strategy, the case study demonstrates the complex nature of explanation and choice making. Students can also learn from each other and participate actively in figuring out answers to problems. Note that the students also have in hand an information sheet on uncertainty reduction theory with references to the textbook and some recommended reading. She also lets the students know that the case is about a former communication major who told this scenario in a focus group she was conducting. Here is the case as it appears on the worksheet handed out in class (see the box on page 75).

We invite you now to think about five theories that constitute primary components of the theoretical perspective of your course. Next, browse Chapter 7 for any resources that might be appropriate for you to review as possible sources to recommend to your students. How can you integrate these selected theories more tightly into the thinking and practice of your students?

A CASE STUDY IN UNCERTAINTY IN WORKPLACE RELATIONSHIPS

Scenario (based on a true story)

A young African American male (Eric) arrives at his job at the restaurant where he waits tables. His hair is perfect because he spent almost an hour styling it. His Caucasian manager (Jim) takes one look at him and says, "Go in the restroom and put some water on that hair to calm it down." Eric is dismayed and then very angry. He can't put water on his hair! "Fixing" this style would take a while and he tells Jim so. Jim dismisses Eric from his shift, and the waiter loses an evening of pay. Within another week Eric (who is very good at his job) quits, complaining that his manager's lack of understanding feels like racism.

Analyze this scenario as a case of uncertainty. Remember, there is no one correct answer in case analysis. Rather, we are using a real-life situation to reflect on possible communication choices for ourselves.

1. What type of cognitive and/or behavioral uncertainty exists for both Eric and Jim?
2. What constraints (role, rules, situation, language, etc.) may be adding to the level of uncertainty?
3. Is racism a viable explanation for the situation, or does uncertainty reduction theory work better?
4. What strategies would you advise both Eric and Jim to use for more effective workplace communication?

VOCABULARY

Teaching the vocabulary of interpersonal communication is as challenging as balancing theory and practice. The common complaint is, "There is just so much vocabulary!" This is true. There are about 350 entries in the glossary of our textbooks, and we use just about all of them over the course of a semester. We would estimate that there are fifty to seventy-five core vocabulary terms that we expect students to have as a working vocabulary when talking about interpersonal communication. The idea of professional jargon versus common sense is one of those tensions that students need to negotiate. Elizabeth's colleague, Jennifer Baker, put this problem in perspective:

> [A difficult pedagogical issue is] helping students to understand that learning about interpersonal communication is the same thing as learning, say, about microbiology. Since they [students] communicate every day and have relationships, when we talk about things, they think they understand them, and then freak out when they don't do well on the tests. There are terms, theories, ideas that they have to associate with the experiences they have had with communication and relationships. Getting them to understand this, and then discuss or write, using the theories and terms, I think is the most difficult for them to understand and then apply. (Personal correspondence, October 21, 2004)

Jennifer's statement helps explain those students who complain, "I already know all this stuff." The academic use of terms is quite different from the lay use of terms. The academic vocabulary is a more precise way to understand the nuances of interpersonal communication. For example, a *transaction* in lay terms is usually a quick business deal in a store or at a bank. But a *transaction* in interpersonal communication vocabulary is deep, shared meaning where partners in a dyad reciprocate behavior. Students have to be told this, but once they begin to use academic vocabulary properly, it changes the way they perceive and act in their relationships.

In an introductory class, it is common to test students' understanding of vocabulary on exams. Elizabeth uses a matching section of twenty vocabulary terms on each major exam to test students on basic vocabulary. So learning the vocabulary terms also helps prepare them for upper-level courses. We need students to be comfortable with such terms as *dyad* and *dialectics*, so we don't mind testing for this as part of their overall assessment of learning. Given how much vocabulary there is, posting vocabulary lists online for students to access and study is a useful technique. During review sessions for exams, and time permitting, a fun activity to play is vocabulary *Jeopardy*: Divide the class into two teams. Read definitions and ask students to call out the answers in the form of questions. For example:

> Instructor: Behaviors that gain the agreement of your partner, persuading him or her to do as you wish. For example, promising dinner if your roommate will help you move some furniture.
>
> Student: What is a compliance-gaining strategy?

We can play *Jeopardy* for fifteen minutes, awarding points to teams, and get the review done in a hurry. Students love the competition, but they also get a sense of what vocabulary is important for the exam, thus enabling them to continue studying on their own. The game also provides much-appreciated levity to the classroom.

For us, one of the challenges in teaching vocabulary is showing students why it is important. We tell them that if they can name an experience, then they can take the next step, which is to talk about that experience in an intelligent manner. This is where we can separate "everyone communicating and having relationships" from "educated people who can communicate with knowledge and make strategic choices for more effective relationships." There is a significant difference.

TECHNOLOGY AND INSTRUCTION

Technology serves as both an instructional strategy and a course structure, depending on your use of it. If you are using technology as an instructional strategy, it supports the course in a different manner than if you are teaching an online course; in the latter case the course and the technology are inseparable. *Low-technology* courses are those in which you can sit in a circle with a small group and get into a discussion that is so meaningful you don't want

class to end. *High-technology* courses are those with constant audio-visual stimulation, including film clips, PowerPoint or Prezi slides, Web sites, and sound
stimulation. Notice that talking about technology in this manner is more about
how technology helps you deliver instruction. If you have more than ten students in a class, you may need some level of technology to deliver information
about interpersonal communication concepts. For example, PowerPoint slides
work well to deliver key points during a lecture. However, visual presentation
expert William Earnest, author of *Save Our Slides*, warns that visual presentations can be too wordy, too simple *or* too complex, and overall too routine. His
suggestions on creating slides could enhance the visuals you use during your
lectures. A scene from a film could demonstrate particular relational concepts
such as *metacommunication* and conflict-management strategies. Web sites are
also helpful. Facebook and Twitter, among others, provide a basis for talking
about Internet friendships and the pros and cons of Internet self-disclosure in
relationships. Students want to talk about the role of technology in their relationships, so it is appropriate to use the Internet as a resource. Instructors may
have different levels of comfort using technology in the instructional process,
but students often expect some technology to be integrated into the course.

Other instructional strategies that are linked to technology include online
discussions and the use of Blackboard to post notes, assignments, or activities
required for the course. Reserve readings are now frequently electronic as well,
so students either read journal articles on a computer screen or print copies
to bring to class. As more students wish to take notes using their laptop computers, or as universities require students to own laptops, it is expected that
instructors will welcome laptops into the classroom. This poses a particular
problem for interpersonal communication instructors, given the preferred
mode of face-to-face interaction and the frequent rearranging of desks for activities. The instructor cannot see a student's face when a computer screen hides
it — therefore, a laptop acts as a nonverbal barrier to interaction. Students often
engage in other activities on their laptops, such as surfing the Internet, completing other assignments, or checking e-mail, and become disengaged from
the class. The clicking sound of keyboards is a distraction for those not using
computers. For all of these reasons, an interpersonal communication instructor
may need to formulate a policy about the use of laptops and tablets and put it
in the syllabus.

SERVICE LEARNING

Service learning is an instructional strategy that has gained popularity in the last
ten years in communication studies. Endorsed by the National Communication
Association (NCA) and linked to both Campus Compact and the American
Association for Higher Education, service learning is generally defined as "a
pedagogy that addresses both our obligations as 'institutional neighbors' in the
communities in which our campuses are located and our historic role of preparing students for participation in civil society" (Droge & Murphy, 1999, p. 3).
James Applegate and Sherry Morreale, both NCA advocates for service learning,

see it as "what happens when students are afforded the opportunity to practice what they are learning in their disciplines, in community settings where their work benefits others" (1999, p. x). There is also a form of critical service learning (Artz, 2001) where a student's service to community is seen as a political act involving a transformative experience between student and community members that helps build social capital (Putnam, 2000) using communication and social action.

In Elizabeth's communication department, they have a commitment to service learning involving twenty to forty hours spent in the community by each student enrolled in a service-learning course. The introductory interpersonal communication course is not designated as service learning; rather, they engage it through a communities course, a research methods course, and an intercultural communication course. In conducting research for this book we did not find service learning to be a widespread instructional strategy in the introductory interpersonal communication course. There may be two reasons for this: First, the majority of courses are taught with a skills-based approach that requires basic practice of competencies best done in familiar dyadic contexts (e.g., family, friendship, romance). Second, the maturity level of the traditional introductory student may not be at a point where service in the community is the best use of his or her time and effort. Service learning is a serious commitment that may require advanced cognitive skills, knowledge sets, and levels of maturity that are more suited for and expected from juniors and seniors.

That is not to say that service learning shouldn't be employed in introductory interpersonal communication courses. Depending on the approach of the course, service learning may be a very appropriate strategy. A course that employs service learning as one instructional strategy rather than the overall structure of the course may work out well to provide a community or field experience that puts theory into practice. A good example is the service-learning component Tasha Souza (1999) developed using a social constructionist perspective. She wanted her students to use dialogue as a way to see how communication creates relationships and social reality (the basic concept of social constructionism). Her students went out into the community to preselected sites for a four-hour experience and then each wrote up a six-page paper that interpreted the communication process he or she engaged in with community members. In particular, students wrote about negotiating selves, perception, expressing self, dialogic listening, and verbal/nonverbal process. Professor Souza's evaluation of the strategy revealed its usefulness in helping students apply interpersonal concepts in the real world, understand the concept of agency in the communication process, and see the value of service learning as a contribution to community.

If you are thinking about service learning as an instructional strategy, consider the following questions:

- Does service learning as an instructional strategy fit with the objectives of the course?
- Do I want to incorporate service learning as one strategy or as the entire approach to the course?

- Does my institution have a service-learning office that could help with arranging service sites and meeting any legal obligations as students travel off campus?
- Are there enough community sites (e.g., homeless shelters, schools) where interpersonal relationship building would be at the core of student activities?
- Do I need resources for supervision of student learning and site visitation?
- What specific assignments (journals, papers, etc.) would be appropriate as an assessment of the learning accomplished through community service?

Finally, plan ahead if you are going to employ service learning. There is a lot of legwork that needs to be done as you prepare the course. Consult the NCA Web site (www.natcom.org) for various resources on service learning. You might want to attend state, regional, or national workshops to help with the preparation of service-learning instruction. If you are a novice teacher, perhaps team teach with a more experienced instructor before going out on your own. All in all, service learning can be one of the most profound learning experiences a college student will ever participate in, so it is worth thinking about how the introductory interpersonal course could contribute to such an experience.

CONCLUSION

This chapter brought up issues about structuring an interpersonal course to successfully deliver its content. There is no one best way to do this, so your challenge is to build instruction that works for you and your students. Use variety, have fun, and get students involved. It's clear that we are way beyond the days of lecturing as the primary method of instruction. Effectiveness in teaching, at least in the introductory interpersonal communication course, is a balance of methods, a balance of theory and practice, a balance of responsibility between teacher and student, and, ultimately, a balance between the teaching and learning processes.

5

Evaluation and Assessment

This chapter focuses on the most difficult aspect of an interpersonal communication course: administering tests and evaluating student progress. The dilemma of grading students is that most of their relating happens outside of class, where we are not present to observe them, thus making it difficult to track competency development. The course has to set up tangible assignments and measurement instruments that enable each student to analyze, apply, and evaluate his or her own performance in relationships. We are often left with knowledge and comprehension as the primary cognitive abilities that we can measure with any degree of certainty. In order to test students' analytical and evaluative skills, instructors need to create both hypothetical and real-world situations; these work fairly well. In addition to giving examinations, assignments that support the learning objectives of the course need to be constructed and graded, and an overall grading system needs to be developed. Further, with most institutions under the mandate of statewide assessment or accrediting procedures, program assessment compliance is now the responsibility of many individual instructors. This chapter examines program assessment procedures and what can be learned under the guidance of the National Communication Association (NCA). It should be noted that evaluation is not based solely on one type of grading, but that learning objectives, general feedback, student evaluation, a grading system, and program assessment are all interconnected. Although we will separate topics for purposes of discussion, keep in mind that everything in this chapter happens as a systemic process.

COURSE STRUCTURE AND LEARNING OBJECTIVES

Recall from Chapter 2 that the syllabus serves as the structural template for the course; learning objectives support the aim and direction of the course. For an introductory course, our best advice is to keep it simple. Elizabeth tells her students:

> The emphasis of the course is on the practical application of concepts and strategies. In addition to gaining knowledge through lecture and reading, students will increase awareness of relational messages through skill-based activity, discussion, and a relationship analysis.

Following are the learning objectives and, in square brackets, the evaluation measures she uses to ensure that those objectives are being met:

GENERAL OBJECTIVES

Upon completion of this course, the student should be able to

1. define and use a vocabulary of relational communication terms
   [evaluated by quizzes, exams, model exercise, and relationship analysis];
2. apply major theoretical concepts in the field of relational communication to real-world relationships
   [evaluated by model exercise, relationship analysis, exams, and in-class exercises];
3. analyze his or her own role in interpersonal relationships in a family, professional, friendship, interracial/intercultural, or intimate context
   [evaluated by relationship analysis, exams, and class discussions];
4. apply both practical and theoretical knowledge to increase his or her own competency in relational communication skills
   [evaluated by in-class exercises, class discussions, quizzes, exams, and competence diary]; and
5. evaluate the effectiveness of an interpersonal relationship
   [evaluated by relationship analysis, class discussions, and in-class exercises].

At the introductory level, much of this course is about building knowledge of vocabulary, concepts, and theories. The skills, or *competencies*, are limited because students are just learning to name behaviors and try out some of the skills in their lives. We both include a lot of application questions on our exams so that students can demonstrate that they understand how a concept should work in a real or hypothetical situation. The hope is that if a student can apply a concept in a hypothetical situation, he or she will be able to apply that concept in a real-life situation. We can't be there in everyday life to evaluate each student's actual competence, so we can at least use exams to determine whether the student is competent and prepared. Our courses are typical of most such courses in schools across the country. Even though we emphasize knowledge and skills, most of us spend more time evaluating through exams rather than by actual observation of skills.

Interpersonal communication course syllabi collected from institutions across the country revealed that performance on exams accounts for anywhere from 25 to 75 percent of the course grade, with about 60 percent as the average. These statistics indicate that we seem to value examinations as a primary form of student evaluation. In rare instances there are no exams. Instead, students may be evaluated on the work they do in journals, group activities, presentations, projects, movie analyses, class discussions, portfolios, or other learning measures. Ultimately, the goal is to conduct an overall assessment of the student's learning process.

At this point, we want you to see that learning objectives, evaluation measures, and the grading system need to be aligned so that the proper weight for each component reflects what you are doing in the course. If your course is speaking-intensive, writing-intensive, service learning, or any other marker type of course, include that as part of the learning objectives and evaluation.

GRADES AND GRADING SYSTEMS

Grading has become more objective over the years. It is no longer acceptable to simply award big red As on papers and exams. Nor can an instructor just add up grades without letting students know the system. Students place enormous value on grades (way more than most teachers) and grade point averages (GPAs). Further, grade inflation is rampant in the American higher education system. Communication courses are particularly subject to this because students have built a mythos about communication as the "easy" major. We do respect that grade inflation is real and student complaints about grades do happen, so we need to be concerned as teachers about what is fair, objective, and appropriate. Most teachers also now use *criterion-referenced* grading systems, in which each student must meet objective criteria set for the course, rather than *norm-referenced* grading systems, in which students are graded against each other.

We suggest you reexamine your university or college policy on grades located in the bulletin or catalog produced by your school. This macro-policy will describe the grading system, the criteria and/or meaning of each grade, and the implications for grades. Procedures for registering complaints about grades should also be mentioned in the policy, as well as in student handbooks and faculty policy manuals. Familiarize yourself with university or college expectations before you create your own grading system and stay within the protocol specified.

The majority of grading systems we have seen for introductory interpersonal communication courses are based on points. All graded activities in the course are listed and assigned a point value. The following is the point system that Elizabeth uses in her course. The actual number of things a student has to do at this level is relatively small, and the items are weighted here to show their relative importance in the overall assessment scheme. Roughly two-thirds of the class material is evaluated by examinations and one-third is activity-based through in-class and out-of-class assignments and exercises.

Quizzes	2 @ 25 pts.	50 pts.	Weight = 13%
Exams	2 @100 pts.	200 pts.	Weight = 54%
Homework		70 pts.	Weight = 20%
Model exercise = 15			
Relationship analysis = 50			
Competence diary = 5			
Class participation and exercises		50 pts.	Weight = 13%
Total		370 pts.	

Students work to earn as many points as possible; the final grade represents some percentage of the total points possible. Most people use a ten-point scale, where 90 to 100 percent of the points earned is an A; 80 to 89 percent of the points earned is a B; and so forth. Not every school requires a particular scale. Elizabeth's school requires the posting of + and – grades because they are calculated into the student's GPA, so the grading scale on her syllabus reflects that. It is also easier to use points when deductions off final point totals are necessary. For example, attendance policies may include point deductions for absence or tardiness. All things considered, points are understood by students and reduce grade complaints because there isn't much to dispute unless a technical error has been made in the grade calculation.

We work hard to set appropriate criteria for student success and to maintain the integrity of the grading system. Admittedly, the negative side to grading is that grades may not reflect what the student actually learned. We evaluate student performance at given moments throughout the semester, but we all know that a student having a "bad semester" may perform below his or her academic capability. Until we invent another system, we maintain the current one.

You also should keep a grade book. Many people prefer computer-generated spreadsheets and post grades for students on Blackboard or other electronic systems. Indeed, today many students prefer to have easy and quick access to their grades through an online format. Using programs like Excel can help with quick input and automatic calculations, and can give you the ability to cut and paste information to send to students. Other professors prefer that students track their own grades and provide space on the syllabus for recording such information. Our universities require electronic posting of the final grade, which allows instructors to post grades quickly and students to access their grades on their own. Alicia likes to provide all options for her students by using Excel, posting grades on Blackboard, and encouraging students to keep track of grades within a chart on the syllabus. She finds that providing multiple locations cuts down on the time it takes to constantly meet with students and update them on their progress. It is also important to consult Family Educational Rights and Privacy Act Regulations (FERPA) to ensure that you are not violating any rules for posting grades. For example, performance expectations range from the length of the assignment to the type of evidence used to supplement the content.

Whether you are grading assignments or exams, you need to set up performance expectations in the instructions you give to students, and then set up the grading criteria to reflect those expectations. For example, performance expectations range from the length of the assignment to the type of evidence or supporting material to be used to content. It is advisable to maintain the integrity of the grading system by giving information out beforehand. Alicia also puts each grading rubric in her course packet that is posted online so that students have a clear understanding of the expectations before the due date. She asks students to print the packet and then goes over each item/point value in the rubric at least one week before the due date. This has helped to increase students' performance on assignments as well as to cut down on student excuses and complaints about grading. The following are general tips for grading that we have learned over the years and that have proven effective.

Tips for Grading

- Blind grade whenever possible to eliminate bias.
- Use a rubric or set of criteria to ensure consistent grading across papers or exams.

- Use an ink color that contrasts with the ink/print on the document so the comments and marks can be seen. (Students generally dislike red in spite of its visibility; you make the call. Alicia likes using purple ink because it shows up nicely, but is not too overwhelming.)
- Grade one item at a time for consistent application of grading criteria. For example, grade all of the number one essay questions at once for consistency and fairness.
- Grade through a set of items or categories and then take a break.
- Shuffle exams periodically so as not to recognize a student's style or fall into an order of grading.
- If writing is important to the presentation of ideas, correct grammar and punctuation.
- Invite the student to come see you if the grade is a D or an F and you detect problems.
- Make comments and notes in the margins. Students expect and appreciate individualized feedback.
- Be sure to balance a lot of positive feedback with your suggestions for improvement. Some suggest a 3 to 1 ratio with more positive comments.
- Spend time grading in proportion to the weight of the assignment.
- Return assignments and exams to students as soon as possible.
- Ask students to wait twenty-four hours before registering a grade complaint.
- Provide a summary of class performance along with the individually graded assignment so students can consider their individual performances in the context of class performance.

EVALUATING CLASS AND HOMEWORK ASSIGNMENTS

Class and homework assignments should measure the progress of a student toward achieving the course's learning objectives. We have our students engage in assessments, exercises, and class discussions as the major forms of activity. Most of this activity involves skill building (e.g., a reflective listening exercise) and application (e.g., constructing Johari Windows for a relationship the student is part of). During class discussion we talk about topics such as strategies for building a positive communication climate in a dyad or conflict management strategies in content and relational conflict situations. We are more global about this type of participation and look for consistency, knowledge/application, and maturity as the student engages us and his or her peers. Elizabeth uses 5 × 8 index cards or assessment sheets from a course packet for most exercises and collects them at the end of the hour. She acknowledges the work with a check system (3, 3+, 3−), writes feedback on every item, and returns it during the next class period. The plus and minus indicate evaluation, while the comments give both evaluation and feedback on their ideas and performance. She keeps notes on class contributions such as frequency and quality of contributions. At the end of the semester, she works out points based on how many items were completed in class over the semester and balances the rest for class contributions. For 50 points worth of class work, her grade book might look like this: class exercises 8 @ 3 points = 24 points; discussion participation then gets the other 26 points. There is a degree of subjectivity here that requires the instructor to use a general rubric for assigning discussion points. For example, in looking at Elizabeth's criteria above, the 26 points would break down as follows:

23–26 points	Student makes a class contribution 28 or more times in a 32-class semester. Student demonstrates excellent knowledge of the concepts and appropriate application. Student makes mature/adult contributions in both content and metacommunication.
20–22 points	Student makes a class contribution 25–27 times in a 32-class semester. Student demonstrates knowledge of the concepts and appropriate application with some misunderstanding at times. Student makes mature/adult contributions in both content and metacommunication the majority of time.
18–19 points	Student makes a class contribution 22–24 times in a 32-class semester. Student shows misunderstanding of knowledge or incorrect application of concepts several times over the semester. Student is mature/adult in contributions most of the time with some breaking of class rules for in-class behavior.
15–17 points	Student makes a class contribution 19–21 times in a 32-class semester. Student consistently shows misunderstanding or incorrect application of concepts. Student frequently breaks class rules and demonstrates immature behavior.
13–14 points	Student makes class contributions less than half the time in a 32-class semester. Student has little to no knowledge of concepts and cannot apply concepts.

	Student consistently breaks class rules, demonstrates immature behavior, and disrupts learning process.
12 points	Student attends class.

Experts such as Rebecca Rubin (1999) advise caution when evaluating participation because it is too subjective and you might penalize a student whose personality you do not like. Alicia thinks that grading participation subjectively in some classes can breed negativity, create unnecessary competition, or privilege the extroverts while some more reticent students are actually quite in tune with the discussion and perform well on exams. However, Elizabeth disagrees with the idea of not evaluating participation in an interpersonal communication class, because the pedagogy is based in active participation. She says, "We communicate to learn!" We recommend you choose the strategy that best fits your teaching philosophy.

Now is a good time to bring up a philosophical issue about evaluation. The traditional way of evaluating students is through a *performance-based* approach — that is, the final grade assesses how well the student performed on course criteria. A newer approach is the *learning-based* philosophy, where the teacher attempts to track the student's cognitive development and maturity as he or she progresses through the course. In his study on teaching excellence, teacher Ken Bain (2004) describes how the best teachers use a learning-based approach, where grades are used to communicate with students rather than rank students' performances:

> Learning entails primarily intellectual and personal changes that people undergo as they develop new understandings and reasoning abilities. . . . Evidence about learning might come from an examination, a paper, a project, or a conversation, but it is that learning, rather than a score, that professors try to characterize and communicate. (p. 153)

Elizabeth has developed a kind of hybrid approach that combines both performance and learning approaches. Look back at the rubric above for evaluating participation as a good example of the hybrid philosophy: There are rewards for numbers of contributions, but the change in learning is evident in the criteria for mature contributions and demonstration of internalized learning. She does look at performance and penalties because students need to continue in that mode after college. In the working world, performance evaluations are common practice. On the other hand, this is the student's education, and Elizabeth believes her job is to help each one learn to be a more competent thinker, a problem solver, and, in the case of the introductory interpersonal course, a more competent relational partner who can use effective communication strategies. We spend a lot of time listening to students in order to perfect the way we teach so that the learning process is the best it can be. Elizabeth does not use extra credit, something that Bain asserts may reflect little on learning and a lot on racking up points. We both spend a lot of time trying to get students to move away from their tendencies to think and act in discrete chunks of knowledge (that is, what is necessary to memorize for a test) and move toward a more holistic thinking and behavioral process. We design essay test questions that take a student in the direction of the big picture (example: "What is the transactional philosophy and how might its implementation contribute to the overall health of an interpersonal relationship?"). We look for this type of thinking and behaving in student participation throughout all course activities.

EVALUATING MAJOR CLASS ASSIGNMENTS

It is useful to use a rubric to evaluate major class assignments because you can create and refine the rubric over time as you continue to use the assignments, and a rubric standardizes evaluation, making it a process that can be applied objectively to all students. According to J. Worth Pickering, assessment director at Old Dominion University, a rubric is a "standardized scoring guide that identifies important criteria and levels of success for each criterion. A rubric describes qualitative as well as quantitative differences" (2006). The most common rubric in our field is the NCA Competent Speaker Speech Evaluation Form. In an entry-level interpersonal communication course, the one activity for which we have a discipline-wide rubric is conversation (Spitzberg, 1995). The Conversational Skills Rating Scale is available through the NCA corporate office. For the most part, you will need to create your own rubric for each major assignment. This is tricky and takes some practice. If you are new at constructing rubrics, look for opportunities to attend assessment workshops, and ask colleagues for help. Meanwhile, two useful Web sites to help you get started are RubiStar, http://rubistar.4teachers.org/index.php, and Stylus Publishing, http://styluspub.com/resources/introductiontorubrics.aspx. Stylus is the publisher of the primer called *Introduction to Rubrics* (Stevens & Levi, 2005), which you may want to order if your library doesn't have a copy.

Elizabeth's students conduct a relationship analysis as their major class assignment and spend about two-thirds of the semester working on it. In this assignment, each student analyzes and evaluates a variety of communication processes in a current relationship in which he or she is a partner. A common alternative to an assignment like this might be to log activities in a journal intended to chart a student's interpersonal communication development over the course of the semester. Her colleague Chris Poulos assigns an in-class partnership project to his students in which they are asked to pair off and develop a dyad using the skills and concepts being taught. These partnerships allow Professor Poulos to teach core skills and to make his own observations of student interpersonal communication. His students all turn in a ten- to twelve-page essay at the end of the partnership to document the assignment. This is a major part of his course and is weighted at 200 points. On the next page is a box containing a completed rubric, with a sample set of points a student might earn on the assignment.

CST 207 POULOS   NAME _____

EVALUATION RUBRIC: Partnership Evaluation Exercise

Scoring:

10 — **Excellent:** Surpasses criteria in terms of complexity and depth — e.g., several examples, thorough consideration, ingenuity. Demonstrates the writer's ability to produce and synthesize complex ideas.

9 — **Very good:** Surpasses criteria in one or more areas in regard to complexity and depth. Demonstrates the writer's ability to produce and synthesize complex ideas and draw on evidence from texts, films, lectures, and discussions. Evidence of minor weaknesses.

8 — **Good:** Meets the listed criteria, offering minimal examples and sufficient evidence of analysis. Demonstrates evidence of the writer's ability to support key ideas, but does not show the highest level of synthesis and complexity.

7 — **Average:** Shows superficial execution of listed criteria. Demonstrates that the writer possesses average ability to support ideas, synthesize information, or analyze issues thoroughly.

6 — **Poor/lowest passing grade:** Does not sufficiently meet listed criteria. Shows several errors in reasoning, little development of ideas, few examples or details, and little evidence.

5 — **Unacceptable/failure:** Fails to meet listed criteria. Shows serious errors in reasoning, little or no development of ideas, and/or few or no details and evidence.

Criteria:

9   *Completeness:* The author offers a direct, specific, detailed, and complete answer to the question or assignment. The author thoroughly explores the theory/concept/theme being examined.

8   *Clarity/Coherence:* The author offers a clear, readable, and compelling presentation of ideas/insights in response to the question or assignment. The various parts of the paper "stick together" — i.e., the paper is marked by an orderly or logical relation of parts that affords comprehension or recognition.

7.5 *Support:* The author supports his/her story/argument with clear examples from everyday communicative life, practical knowledge, class discussions, etc., and provides textual support from course texts, films, class lectures, etc.

9   *Application:* The author carefully explores and explains how the theory/concept/theme under examination applies to his/her and others' communicative lives.

8   *Professional Presentation:* The author writes a polished paper with no grammatical, spelling, or typographical errors. Citations are made in appropriate style format (APA, MLA), and a reference list/bibliography is provided.

41.5 TOTAL POINTS ÷ 5 (CATEGORIES) = 8.3 (AVG) = 166/200 POINTS = B-LETTER GRADE

EXAMINATIONS

Test Construction

Examinations are a typical component of most courses and they serve to evaluate each student's performance at given points in the semester. They are only one type of measurement of a student's overall learning. New teachers, graduate assistants, or teachers participating in a standardized course created by the department may use tests provided by senior teachers, a departmental test bank, or the instructor's manual that accompanies a textbook. Test banks can be extremely helpful, but be sure that the questions are clear and that they fit your way of teaching the ideas presented. If you teach a lesson with a slightly different interpretation than the text, sometimes the wording of test bank items can be confusing for students. However, if you are not subject to a testing policy or use of particular standardized tests, then you probably create your own. Test construction, like the creation of learning objectives, is a highly technical process and one that most people cannot do well without some kind of instruction. Because constructing and testing an exam for reliability and validity are difficult, it is not recommended that you constantly create new exams. Having a template with interchangeable items that can be switched out or added works well. We also use all types of test questions, from true/false to essays, because the entry-level course typically has younger students who are making the transition from straight objective-type questions such as multiple-choice to the more interpretive-type questions such as essays. We are helping students go from comprehension to synthesis and evaluation in their critical thinking skills, and the exams reflect this progression. Also, different types of questions work efficiently to measure different types of knowledge—for example, matching questions for vocabulary terms and multiple-choice for application of concepts.

It takes a while to fine-tune quizzes and exams, so we could not completely teach test construction skills here. We will offer two pieces of advice: First, a test should have integral links to course learning objectives, the knowledge set under study, and the appropriate levels of Bloom's taxonomy (Bloom, 1956; Krathwohl, 2002; see discussion in Chapter 2). If those three items are not aligned, then there isn't much point in using an exam as part of the overall assessment of a student's learning. Second, if you cannot take a course in test construction (and we highly recommend it), then teach yourself the basic philosophy and mechanics by reading the sources in this chapter's reference list by L. B. Curzon (2004, Chapters 29 and 30), Rebecca Rubin (1999), and Neil Salkind (2006). These three sources provide explanations of basic terminology; how to consider reliability and validity; how to write test items of all types, including true/false, multiple-choice, matching, short-answer, and essays; how to format; tips on grading; and the pros and cons of the many decisions you need to make when constructing an exam that is right for your course. We suggest buying the textbook used in the test construction course taught in your teacher education program and perhaps even asking the professor of that course for some advice. A text that has helped us is *Measurement and Evaluation in Teaching* (Gronlund & Linn, 1990). Such a text will take you through the entire process of linking your learning objectives to the test you are constructing to long-term appraisal of your test.

Preparing Students

Students should begin their own preparation for quizzes and tests by knowing from the first day of class exam policies and dates for testing, as published on the syllabus. We remind students of the big concepts to expect on a test (e.g., "You will need to synthesize your own view of the transactional philosophy and be able to articulate that on the first quiz") so they are not surprised. Several days before the exam we conduct an in-class review in which we list on the board the types of questions (T/F, matching, etc.) and the point values for each of the question types. Alicia provides a review sheet online at least one week before the exam with examples of sample questions that might be in each section of the test. Elizabeth puts Bloom's taxonomy on the board and shows what types of cognitive skill go with different sections of the test. For example, because of the sheer volume of vocabulary, she includes a matching section of vocabulary terms and definitions. Students know that these are about knowledge and comprehension levels. Multiple-choice questions test a student's ability to comprehend and apply concepts. By the time they reach the essay portion of the exam, they see that they need to be prepared to analyze, synthesize, and evaluate theories such as social exchange, uncertainty reduction, and attribution in interpersonal situations.

Then, we talk about how to study for different types of test questions. We show students how to use the syllabus as a template for content and progression of thought about concepts as they study. Guiding students to the end-of-chapter reviews in the textbook is also helpful for a quick overview of the reading. Additionally, we like to spend some class time clarifying concepts or filling in the holes in students' notes before the exam. We also remind students of our availability through office hours and let them know that they can e-mail for last-minute questions. In addition to making ourselves available, we also encourage students to pair up with a study-buddy or make sure they have another student's contact information before leaving the class. Some instructors like to do in-class review games such as Jeopardy or Bingo to help students prepare for the exam. On the downside, these games take quite a bit of advance preparation on your part, and they may not actually help students absorb the material when it is mentioned so briefly during the exam; yet you might want your students to have fun and enjoy a day of something different, and it might serve as a wake-up call to those more unprepared students. Finally, it's important to remind students to bring their Scantron forms and No. 2 pencils, along with a pen if they prefer that for essays. This will cut down on time spent searching for exam materials, and allow students to calmly focus on their test.

Test Administration

The basic protocol for administering tests is designed to provide an atmosphere conducive to test taking and to minimize cheating. Students do cheat when

---

FROM THE CLASSROOM: Cheating in the Large Enrollment Course

I think the biggest logistical challenge is actually conducting the exams in the allotted amount of time with the allotted amount of space with very few proctors. Cheating is typically occurring and we catch what we can, but I know we are missing a lot. It would be nice to be able to break into smaller sections, but we don't have the resources/proctors to do it. One of the strategies we use for dealing with cheating (people who are looking at other people's exams) is that we announce we will move you if you are looking at someone else's test, or if we think someone is looking at your test — this way it is less face threatening in a large group. We also now don't let students leave the room once they have a test (before I started doing this I had students go into the bathrooms with their cell phones).

Kelly Morrison
Michigan State University

SOURCE: Personal correspondence with Elizabeth Natalle, June 6, 2006.

---

given the opportunity. We found this out the first year we taught, and research over the years consistently supports that finding — and that students cheat a lot. Our favorite discovery in the past couple of years is the way students store vocabulary and information in their cell phones and then attempt to access that with their cell phones in their laps during tests. In a class with a large enrollment, the task of monitoring cheating is the number one concern. Below, Kelly Morrison of Michigan State University talks about cheating in her team-taught course, which enrolls just over 650 students, with only one teaching assistant assigned to the team.

To reduce cheating during exams:

- If feasible, seat students one seat apart in a row and make students move desks to increase space.
- Ask students to put all personal belongings under their desks, with only their writing instruments and Scantron/computer forms on the desktop.
- Ask students to put cell phones on a table in the front of the classroom and provide sticky notes for the students to label their phones with their names.
- Hand out exams individually to students so that you can glance around on the floor, the desks, and around the students' personal belongings.
- Provide the paper for the exam so students do not need to have extra paper on their desks. (Both blue books and laptop computers can come preloaded with information.)
- Walk around the room during the exam and walk very close to any student you suspect is cheating. If the room is too small for movement, scan it with your eyes and smile if you make eye contact with a student.

- Do not leave the room; it is recommended that students not be allowed to leave during the exam either. If you do allow students to leave the room, then let only one student at a time go to the restroom.
- Bring tissues to prevent extra reasons for students to leave the room.
- Do not get caught up in conversation with students turning in exams. Maintain quiet and order for those still writing.
- If students reveal cheating by other students or you catch students cheating, follow the policies on your syllabus and at your university to take action.
- Don't let students keep exams. After going over the exam results, students should turn exams back in; be sure that all exams are returned.

If you administer exams through the computer, ask your campus testing center how to put safeguards in place. The university should have procedures in place if students go to a center to take exams.

Other procedural items include giving time checks and bringing extra pencils and Scantron/computer forms to class. Give instructions if necessary and be available to clarify any questions a student may have (some still don't read the printed directions on an exam and then ask questions about what to mark on the Scantron form versus the test paper itself). If you have a blind student, a student with a hand in a cast, a student who needs extra time because of a learning disability or English as a second language, or any other logistical issue, make arrangements to proctor that exam elsewhere and agree in advance to a plan with the student. Are you feeling anxious and paranoid as you read all of this protocol? Don't be. Go into the room early on test days, be organized, be friendly and calm in attitude, and be helpful to students. All of this relieves stress for everyone. Elizabeth tells her students that exams should actually be great days because it is their opportunity to shine and "show me their stuff." They usually laugh, but we do think being positive about taking exams is a good approach. Alicia has even brought candy Smarties in for exam time to provide a little encouragement. (Note: Dum-Dum suckers send the wrong message.)

Grading Tests and Debriefing Students

Follow the tips described earlier in the chapter to be consistent, efficient, and fair when grading an examination. Prepare scoring keys before you start grading, and make notes on the way students interpret short-answer and essay questions. If you locate errors, go back and correct every test item just to be fair. Double-check the computer for scoring errors. Score all parts of the exam in sections. Add numbers and arrive at a grade when you are fresh and thinking clearly. If you are constructing a new exam or trying out new items, conduct an item analysis. Alicia always looks through the item analysis of each question to see if there were certain questions missed by at least 50 percent of the class. This analysis indicates how many students answered with option A, B, C, and so forth. Then, she looks back at the question to determine if the question was misleading, confusing, or simply a "reader question" in which the students failed to take the time to look through the book and instead relied on lecture material only. She also notes questions with 100 percent correct answers because these questions were likely not challenging enough and should be removed for future exams. Computer-scored exams can sometimes provide item analyses, but if you need to do it yourself, you might consult a source like Neil Salkind (2006), who provides formulas for computing difficulty indices, discrimination indices, and reliability and validity checks.

We both spend time handing back exams (during the last twenty to thirty minutes of the next class period) and going over everything. Class performance information is put on the test analysis form we give back so students can see how they performed as both individuals and as a class. In spite of criterion-referenced grading, students engage in a lot of social comparison and want to know where they stand in relation to their peers. We tell our students that we blind grade. We also say that we will not argue questions or grades from individual students in front of the whole class. Any student with a grade dispute should come to our office for private consultation. This debrief includes providing correct answers, letting students know which items the class had difficulty with, and why a given correct answer is what it is. Keep in mind that exams are also a time for you to assess *your* teaching as well as their learning. Thus, you should note privately those items for information on what to reteach if students appear not to have met your learning goals. For short essays, Elizabeth likes to praise four to five people who met the criteria by saying something like, "John, Megan, Keshia, Joel, and Hollie did a great job on this essay. Megan, why don't you read your answer to us so we can hear what the question was looking for in a good response?" In this way, students hear their classmates meeting the expectations of the exam question and can rethink their own strategies for the next exam.

Because we collect the exams after the debrief, we give each student a test analysis form to fill out and keep in their notebook. Students are also invited to come to our office at any time and visit their exams on file. If a student clearly indicates poor test-taking skills, we put a note on his or her exam inviting an office visit to strategize. We then go over missed items and talk about different ways to think in the privacy of a tutorial session. If a student flat out fails an exam (sometimes we know why and sometimes we don't), we will put a personal note to this effect: "I know this isn't your best work. Come see me and we will strategize." Or, if there were challenging circumstances outside the classroom, we might write, "I know you've had a tough time lately. You will do better next time. Come see me if you need help." In each case, there is an acknowledgment of a problem, a show of empathy, and an invitation to help the student improve. Finally, we ask the student to set a goal if he or she wants to make a different grade on the next exam and to record what to work on in preparation for the next exam. Alicia also encourages her students to come back to her office and revisit previous exams right before an upcoming exam so that they can reacquaint themselves with the style of questions and discuss studying pitfalls as

---

CST 207 EXAM 1 ANALYSIS

Name: _____   **Class Performance:**

n=33

Grade: T/F & Mult. Choice _____ out of 45   Range = 36–94
      Matching _____ out of 20   Average = 78 Median   = 80
      Essay _____ out of 35   Grade cutoff: 90–100   =A [5]*
                                    80–89   =B [13]
                                    70–79   =C [8]
Total _____ out of 100   60–69   =D [5]
                                    59–below =F [2]

* The number in brackets equals the number of people in our class who made this grade. You can see that the overall performance of the class was good and, in fact, a nice bell curve. These are good grades overall, and everyone is in good shape.

Tips for the entire class: Most of the problems were on the essays and vocabulary. On the essays, read the question carefully and provide a relevant answer. Rather than telling me everything you know about a topic, answer with the essential information. Draw conclusions and answer all parts of the question. Take time to write coherent sentences that are grammatically correct. This class has a good imagination, so combine your creative examples with solid theory and you'll do great on the next exam. See Dr. Natalle if you need help, want something clarified, or just plain need to talk about your test performance if it was not your usual grade.

What areas or test strategies are you going to work on to improve your score on the next exam?

---

well as ways to improve on the upcoming exam. A sample of an analysis form the student keeps is shown above, with actual information from a test given in class.

Mini-Assessment

For a final note on assessment, keep in mind the idea of "mini-assessment." While the goal of assessment is to determine what your students are learning and retaining, exams should not be the only ways of assessing your students. Beyond papers, presentations, and other major assignments, consider mini-assessments on a daily basis for determining students' understanding. Offering other small means of assessing knowledge through small quizzes and daily free-writes gives you a chance to see what your students know before they are faced with a heavily weighted exam. Giving students other means of assessment along the way helps build your relationship with them and helps them see your assessment style. You can consider offering quizzes and free-writes that are graded, non-graded, or for participation only. The goal is just for students to determine where they need to improve their efforts in the class before the big exam day. It also helps the instructor figure out where you need to refresh the material or clear up misunderstandings. For a great resource on a variety of means for assessing your students, see the book *Classroom Assessment Techniques: A Handbook for College Teachers* (2nd ed.) written by Thomas Angelo and K. Patricia Cross. Their book provides easy step-by-step instructions for administering a variety of assessments in the classroom.

ASSESSMENT

Program Assessment

In Chapter 2 we spent time discussing assessment as a nationwide phenomenon. In some ways the assessment movement is modeled after the way high schools are mandated to test for student learning. In higher education the pressure is on from state legislators to assess whether students are learning what we say we are teaching them. In a communication studies program, the interpersonal communication course *may* play a role in a department's systematic assessment program. We say *may* because introductory courses are not necessarily sites for measuring student learning. Senior-level and capstone courses are more likely a part of assessment, but if you only have one interpersonal communication course, you may be required to participate.

Our point in the earlier discussion was to show how course learning objectives relate to assessment learning outcomes. We want to extend that discussion just a bit in this chapter, but before you read further, you might want to revisit the discussion on assessment in Chapter 2 (p. 36). Then review the NCA Web site's assessment resources to familiarize yourself with their perspective, at www.natcom.org. The NCA site is very informative and provides a thorough crash course in a short period of time. We highly recommend that you spend the time to gain both knowledge and context on the topic. Finally, if you want to gain some historical grounding for the way the communication discipline responded to the assessment movement, read Bill Christ's edited anthology, *Assessing Communication Education* (1994). This was the first comprehensive resource guide produced in this discipline and it covers all the important topics.

The NCA has a list of suggested interpersonal communication competencies that majors should be proficient in if they expect to function effectively beyond college. You can find these basic interpersonal competencies on the NCA Web site at www.natcom.org/Secondary.aspx?id=119&terms=interpersonal%20 competencies (from the homepage, go to The Teaching and Learning Tab, then to Virtual Faculty Lounge, then to Assessment Resources).

The basic skills include achievement in speaking and listening in interpersonal contexts as well as those that we would expect college graduates to use as part of their professional communication and in their citizenship. These skills may be included in both entry-level and advanced-level interpersonal communication courses. You may want to think about the competencies from three perspectives: what you need to assess as part of your communication program; whether your learning objectives for your course dovetail with the standards of expectation developed by our professional organization; and which assignments in your course may serve both as evaluation measures of student progress and as vehicles for assessing student accomplishment of program learning outcomes. Very often, administrators appreciate that course instructors are taking into consideration a discipline-specific set of skills endorsed by the profession.

Consider how program assessment may play a role in how you set up learning objectives and choose evaluation measures for your interpersonal communication course. It's a good idea to consult with your department head and university or college assessment office to ensure that you comply with the institution's assessment plan. Guidance from the National Communication Association can help you match your school's learning outcomes with professional expectations developed by the discipline.

Teacher Assessment

We are a performance-behavioral-oriented discipline, and as professional communicators, we are expected to model what we teach. However, performance without content is not good teaching, and we do need to assess ourselves as teachers. Typically we are assessed by means of student evaluations, peer evaluations of teaching, formal mentoring, self-assessment, and alumni evaluations. Each type of evaluation may be used or weighted differently in your overall performance evaluation.

We think our discipline has done a good job of addressing this issue and our literature reflects a range of good sources, from Katherine Hendrix's (2000) mention in her teaching assistant training guide to Anita Vangelisti's (1999) comprehensive chapter on assessing teaching process. Pamela Cooper and Cheri Simonds are now on the seventh edition of their book, *Communication for the Classroom Teacher* (2003), an excellent source for motivating new teachers to practice the kind of interpersonal skills that lead to positive teacher evaluations. *Communication Education* has also published consistently on the implications of teacher behavior on student evaluations of teacher performance, including teacher immediacy (Moore, Masterson, Christophel, & Shea, 1996), teacher caring (Teven & McCroskey, 1997), teachers' aggressive communication (Schrodt, 2003), and halo effects of teacher behavior (Feeley, 2002). Communication research reveals that competent relating produces high teaching evaluations, yet it takes hard work to get to the point where you are not either worrying over your own performance evaluations or teaching to the items on the teaching evaluation forms. To that end, we like the advice that Kalamazoo Valley Community College professor Marion Boyer gives to new teachers of interpersonal communication:

Be the interpersonal communicator the textbooks describe. Every movement, gesture, expression, sentence, glance of yours should model what is best practice in interpersonal communication. You're their human textbook. Then, be aware that you, too, have much to learn. Interpersonal communication is a process, and we're all evolving. Let the students know you're willing and eager to evolve right along with them. (Personal correspondence with Elizabeth Natalle, April 26, 2006)

This is healthy advice that should help you grow and earn high evaluations for good teaching.

CONCLUSION

This chapter examined the topics of student evaluation measures such as assignments and examinations, grading, and program and teacher assessment. Much of the preparation needed for success is technical in nature, such as learning to conduct reliability checks on your own exams, so we could only take a surface look at best practices. We also considered the challenges of the evaluation and assessment process. We will now turn to Chapter 6 for an exploration of teaching interpersonal communication courses online.

Teaching Resources

6

Teaching Online Courses in Interpersonal Communication

Guest co-author: Jocelyn DeGroot,
Southern Illinois University Edwardsville

When given the opportunity to teach an online, or even hybrid, interpersonal communication course, you may have a lot of thoughts running through your mind: Do I have the expertise to use the technology? Will the technology fail at a critical time? Will students learn as much, or more, from the online course as they do with the traditional face-to-face course? Will students enjoy the online experience? You may feel nervous or excited or both about having the opportunity to try the course in a new format with a very difficult schedule. Whether you are contemplating teaching an online class for the first time or are looking for fresh inspiration after teaching interpersonal communication online several times, this chapter aims to enhance your teaching effectiveness in online formats.

Even if you are not teaching online courses, many concepts discussed in this chapter can be useful if you are teaching Web-enhanced courses. There are courses that use some online aspects for information dissemination, such as posting a reading to Blackboard or holding an online discussion. Another option for integrating online strategies is to develop a hybrid class. A hybrid class meets face-to-face at points throughout the semester, and the students also complete some assignments or activities online. Alicia has experimented with hybrid classes for a variety of interpersonal courses and discovered many benefits of online courses. For example, online asynchronous discussion done through the class's Blackboard page has added great depth to students' understanding of interpersonal topics. These discussions are prompted by both student-generated discussion questions and instructor-generated discussion questions, ensuring a variety of topics are covered. Further, she often uses what she calls the "HELP! Board," in which students can post follow-up questions to in-class lectures. These follow-up questions help her see what points need clarification from a previous lecture and provide the students with immediate help rather than letting their confusion linger. Students also use the HELP! Board to ask personal questions that are related to course topics. This allows Alicia the chance to provide her students with research-based answers to their actual relationship challenges.

We'd like to welcome a special contributor to this chapter: Jocelyn DeGroot from the Department of Applied Communication Studies at Southern Illinois University Edwardsville. Josie studies Computer-Mediated Communication (CMC) and interpersonal communication and teaches online and hybrid/blended courses at SIUE. Her experiences teaching online and her research interests provide great insight and advice to our discussion, and we thank her for sharing them with us.

In this chapter we will highlight the benefits of teaching interpersonal communication in online formats; differences between online interpersonal courses and face-to-face courses; strategies for engaging online learners; suggestions for course development, organization, and grading; challenges of teaching interpersonal courses online; and follow-up with additional notes and advice.

BENEFITS OF TEACHING INTERPERSONAL COMMUNICATION ONLINE

Online courses offer many benefits for instructors, students, and the institution. The most obvious is that online courses allow instructors and students to learn together, regardless of the time or day. But that is far from the only perk.

Instructors benefit from teaching online courses in a variety of ways. To begin, teaching online allows instructors flexible use of their time. They can develop their course materials from home in their pajamas — or even in a hotel room! However, online courses are still time-consuming. Indeed, many of the instructors that we talked to about teaching interpersonal communication online suggested that it can be more time-consuming than their traditional face-to-face courses. Amber Schmisseur, adjunct instructor in the Department of Applied Communication Studies at Southern Illinois University Edwardsville and adjunct instructor teaching online courses for Rasmussen College, stated:

> If someone was teaching interpersonal communication online for the first time, I would first warn them that it is a lot of work. In some ways, teaching online takes up much more time than teaching in person.[1]

Although grading online can be time-consuming and the role of the online instructor requires a consistent presence, instructors who teach online do point out the value of being able to teach from locations other than a specific classroom or office and of the opportunities to interact with students in a variety of ways — a student who is quiet in class may be much more comfortable contributing to a discussion board.

The benefits of online courses for students are numerous. Just like instructors, students appreciate the flexibility of online courses as they can schedule around their personal and professional obligations. Further, online courses can enhance student learning. For example, if course lectures are recorded, students can re-watch them as many times as they would like to better understand the material. Or, if the online format allows for asynchronous learning, students can go through the learning modules at their own pace. Other course formats

---

[1] Personal correspondence with Alicia Alexander, November 21, 2013.

may allow real-time, synchronous participation such as Blackboard Collaborate, which allows for live class discussions similar to those in face-to-face classrooms as well as short recorded lectures. Moreover, the one-on-one real time interaction with the instructor can improve some students' learning because they can get the assistance they need from their instructor sooner rather than later, while preventing some frustration and fatigue in the student (Finkelstein, 2006).

Online courses can also support self-directed or proactive learners. This type of learning is initiated by students who are self-paced, independent, and inclined to take their own initiatives in learning. Generally, we find that proactive learners are more successful in online classes than are passive learners. Proactive learners are those who want to learn and become actively involved in the learning process (Pilling-Cormick & Garrison, 2007). For example, a proactive learner is the type of student who would take it upon him- or herself to find additional online sources on the topic "adult attachment styles" when discussing a fear of intimacy in romantic relationships.

An added benefit to online instruction is that it can provide students with up-to-date research and examples on interpersonal communication. Just imagine the current events, latest YouTube videos, Twitter feeds, and Facebook posts that you can integrate into your online course. You can find real-world examples to link to important interpersonal concepts as the news is unfolding. Or what about integrating the latest, just off the presses, journal article on computer-mediated communication within your online discussions? In many ways, online material can be more current and relevant than the material your students usually find in their textbooks.

With completely online courses, the school usually saves on overhead, as they do not need to pay for classroom space and the utilities to run the classroom. However, the school does need to provide increased faculty and technical support, and there may be an initial investment if the school doesn't already provide an online course platform. Institutions can also benefit financially because they can utilize online courses to retain students over the summer rather than having their students return to their hometowns, where they might choose to take a course at the local college and transfer the credits.

DIFFERENCES BETWEEN ONLINE AND FTF

It goes without saying that there are several differences between teaching face-to-face (FTF) interpersonal communication courses and online interpersonal communication courses. So, what differences would you expect? To begin, much of the interaction in an online class is asynchronous in nature, meaning that it doesn't actually happen in real time. This means while you are sitting at your computer working on your class, you will miss some of the unplanned conversations that are likely to occur when you are actually on campus. You won't have the opportunity to help a group of students studying out in the hallway a couple of hours before your exam. Or have a chance encounter with a student on the way into or out of class. As suggested by Finkelstein (2006), since these unplanned conversations are unavailable, online teachers must heavily rely on course materials, reading assignments, and independent learning instead. This can be challenging for motivating both instructors and students if either of you craves the energy of face-to-face interaction.

Another difference is that online courses emphasize written words and text materials more than do face-to-face courses. This requires a lot of work on your part to develop very clear and detailed instructions, definitions, insights, and so forth. However, in asynchronous interactions, instructors and students have time to write, edit, and reflect on their materials and responses before submitting them, so take advantage of this time to make sure everything is as coherent as possible (Smith, Ferguson, & Caris, 2001). A common misconception is that online courses are *always* asynchronous, where the students and instructor are not online at the same time. This is not always true. Some learning management software allows for synchronous, real-time interaction between the instructor and students. If specific online meeting times are required of the students, be sure that the students are aware of these times and the course schedule.

The online disinhibition effect also affects our online communication (Suler, 2004). This concept says that people say and do things on the Internet that they would not ordinarily say and do in the face-to-face world. This can result in both positive and negative communication in your interpersonal communication classes. For example, students might say harsh or rude things online — in discussion boards or in e-mails to you. When teaching online, watch out for signs of disrespectful behavior and directly address any instances that occur. It is best to discuss inappropriate behavior with students individually first to give them the opportunity to improve their behavior without humiliation. Additionally, you can remind students of appropriate classroom communication by posting discussion guidelines and recommendations for all to see. On the other hand, the same feelings of anonymity that make people discourteous might also help them overcome their shyness and encourage them to participate in online discussions.

Because the Internet can allow for equal participation in a discussion or small-group project, students might be more willing to debate ideas or even challenge the instructor (in productive and unproductive ways). Sometimes students can become overly assertive to the point of aggression and question the instructor's authority. When this happens it is best to send correspondence directly to the student, indicating the appropriate behavior expected for online discussion and reiterating policies in the syllabus. However, one of the benefits is that class participation is higher in online classes as multiple students can "speak" at the same time, and the instructor can return to the discussion archive when grading. As mentioned by Amber Schmisseur:

> Teaching interpersonal communication online allows for students who would not otherwise speak up to share their thoughts on a topic. It also brings in people from across the country with various backgrounds and at differing ages. This allows for multiple perspectives, which is something you don't always get from a live lecture class. I have even seen one person talk about a problem they are hav-

ing with their child, and another person offer advice because they experienced the same situation 10 years ago.[2]

Yet, in face-to-face courses, a small percentage of students can participate in discussions due to time constraints (Smith, Ferguson, & Caris, 2001).

LEARNING APPROACHES FOR ONLINE COURSES

It is important to consider the ways in which students can approach their learning when enrolled in an online interpersonal communication course. First, keep in mind that online learning is often considered nonlinear. In the traditional interpersonal communication course on campus, students usually learn chronologically as the material progresses in a linear fashion throughout the semester (Bender, 2003). In contrast, in online courses, students have the opportunity to learn in a nonlinear way due to the layout of the discussion threads on the course's Web site. Think about the way you may have responded to a discussion board in a class that you have either taken or taught. You probably engaged in a threaded conversation in which your message was attached to a comment; thus, your comment was likely arranged by that particular theme, not necessarily chronologically. For many students this is an advantage because they enjoy having the ability to hop in and out of threads without having to follow a linear pattern. This is likely very similar to the conversations they have with their friends on Facebook or on blogs or other message boards where they have the opportunity to jump in and out of conversations. This type of approach is typical of an asynchronous environment, and many students will find they can learn a lot from the nonlinear approach.

It is important to note that some students may struggle with the nonlinear learning approach in an online interpersonal class. Tisha Bender, author of *Discussion-Based Online Teaching to Enhance Student Learning: Theory, Practice and Assessment* (2003), recommends that you remain mindful of the challenges of nonlinear thinking. For instance, if you link to other materials and have students click away from the primary course site, they can access a wealth of additional information on any interpersonal topic. However, this extra clicking is not without its challenges. Students can easily get distracted and overwhelmed by all of the extra information. Bender (2003) says, "I think the question arises as to just how much clicking should we invite our students to do, before they become too disoriented, too dizzy, too remote from the place that is their online class?" As with any decisions you make in developing your online class, you must consider what the best approach is to helping them learn and remain engaged with the material.

A second consideration when developing an online interpersonal communication class is the general pacing of the information that you provide for your students. Bender (2003) advises that online classes not be self-paced. She argues that material should be revealed throughout the semester as it would in

---

[2]Personal correspondence with Alicia Alexander, November 21, 2013.

a face-to-face course. Some learning management systems allow you to issue a delayed release for lectures, weekly modules, and assignments. This can help you set the pace for the course so students have to complete the module each week, rather than three in a week or all at the end of the semester (which can be very overwhelming for even the most motivated self-learner). In addition, until the online course is established and all kinks are worked out, you do need to be flexible in meeting the needs of the students. If you realize that you assigned too many readings or required too many discussion board posts, you will want to change that. If you haven't revealed all modules or lessons in advance, this is easy to do without disrupting students who may have gone ahead in the lessons.

SETTING UP AN ONLINE COURSE

Too often we have heard students taking online courses in a variety of disciplines complain that the course was "too easy," "too boring," "a waste of time," or was just "overwhelming with too much information." Yet, the goal of teaching Web-based courses is to create a course that is as good as (or even better!) than traditional face-to-face formats. After all, a little planning and smart decision making can ensure that online courses are a wonderful learning and teaching experience. To begin, it is crucial that instructors do not conceptualize their online class in the same manner as their face-to-face classes. Instructors must consider important aspects of setting up an online course such as timing and deadlines, creating Internet-friendly activities, and developing online exams. It is key to remember that a lot of the work must be completed *before* the course even begins.

Important Material to Include

Since some students may not have taken an online course before or may have had varying experiences in other online courses, it is important that you provide students with your approach to the course and your expectations upfront. In Josie's online syllabi, she includes the following statement:

> This is an online course in which all of the coursework will be completed online and not in the traditional, physical classroom. You are responsible for keeping up with deadlines throughout the semester. Blackboard will be utilized for this course. Grades, supplemental materials, and class announcements will be posted here. You can download and complete ungraded Reading Notes (available on Blackboard) to help focus your reading of the assigned materials. I will post brief lectures on each chapter to help your understanding of the reading. You will identify artifacts to illustrate course concepts and apply what you read to real-life examples. You will also complete an analysis paper, comparing information in a popular press article to academic research. All assignments are due online through Blackboard. I will post grades on Blackboard within three days of the assignment deadline.

This information should be e-mailed to the students prior to the course or prominently posted on your learning management system (e.g., Blackboard or

WebCT). You should also include basic information about navigating the course and where students can find the materials they need to be successful in the course. Remember to also include contact information for technical support so the students can contact that department for computer troubleshooting.

Because nonverbal cues such as vocal emphasis and gestures are reduced in an online environment, nearly every aspect of your course should be explained in detail to avoid confusion. This includes being very clear about assignment direction and rubrics, how to access certain parts of your course, and course policies. You might even consider providing a transcript of your lectures as well in order to give students the opportunity to have your exact words.

Office hours should also be clearly posted and emphasized. These can be held virtually—via Blackboard Collaborate, Skype, or similar synchronous formats. Students will want, and often need, to have that same personal interaction with you that they could get in a traditional classroom or in traditional face-to-face office hours. In addition to online office hours, we've had students request face-to-face meetings as well. If your students (or a bulk of them) are geographically local, you can consider setting up a few in-person office hours and appointments throughout the semester. This information should be posted to the learning management system (LMS) as well. Because of the 24/7 nature of the Internet, students may expect you to be available at all hours of the day or night and to respond to e-mails or texts immediately. Yet, of course you have other work obligations and personal interests to attend to and you can't be as readily available as other online sources! Indicating your availability and expected e-mail turn-around time will help alleviate these student concerns.

As in a traditional face-to-face course, you also want to clearly state your learning objectives and how you will assess students based on them. You can include this with the syllabus or posted separately on the LMS. Most systems provide a prominent place for your syllabus and course calendar. To ensure the students read and understand your syllabus, you might want to consider creating a graded syllabus quiz that assesses their understanding of specific policies, assignments, and so forth.

Policies

In addition to the usual policies on your syllabus (such as those related to late work, reasonable accommodation, or academic integrity), you'll also want to include policies specifically pertaining to the online context. Josie uses Turnitin for longer paper submissions, so she includes the following policy on her syllabus:

> By taking this course, you agree that all required papers may be subject to submission for textual similarity review to Turnitin for the detection of plagiarism. Some papers submitted for review will be included as source documents in the global Turnitin repository to be used in future reviews. You should remove your name and any other personally identifying information from your papers prior to submission to Turnitin. For additional information on and instructions pertaining to Turnitin, consult the SIUE Turnitin resource page at: www.siue.edu/its/turnitin/

Troubleshooting/Tech Difficulties

You will also want to include information about the procedure that students should follow if they encounter technical difficulties. After all, you are the course instructor, not the IT department, and without a clear notice on whom students should contact, you may end up fielding a lot of support questions that are better directed elsewhere. Josie's policy reads:

> Your SIUE e-mail address will be used for communication purposes. It is your responsibility to check Blackboard and your e-mail regularly. If you have technical difficulties, please contact the help desk at 555-555-5555. They are also available at www.siue.edu/its/bb/. If you have a technical issue during an assignment submission, it is your responsibility to take a screenshot of the issue and email it to me along with your completed assignment. Computer problems or a poor Internet connection are not excuses for failing to complete your work.

While there are numerous ways to set up your online course organization, it is generally best to organize it in week-by-week folders, so students do not need to check five different tabs or tools (e.g., discussion board, quizzes, readings) in order to see if something is due for that week. For example, in Josie's Week 3 folder, she has links to her recorded lecture on Perception, reading notes, a reading quiz, and an application blog. Links to online articles, external quizzes (such as a personality quiz), and videos could also be included in the weekly folders.

Setting up the course early allows students to look through the course and general assignments to determine if it is a manageable workload for them before the semester even starts. This allows for greater student retention in the course.

Bulletin Board/Announcements Page

Whether teaching a hybrid or purely online interpersonal communication course, it is useful for both you and your students to have a Bulletin Board or Announcements page. Bender (2003) recommends that the bulletin board is helpful because it can serve as an in-between virtual spot that can point students to other places and give the most updated course information. This page can be updated at regular intervals to keep students in the loop on assignments, upcoming events, course-related material in the media, and so forth. Students will appreciate the organization and structure that a bulletin board can provide. Further, the board can be used for up-to-date announcements, such as changes in the schedule, class cancelations, information on upcoming campus events, and so forth.

A welcome announcement is a great first post for the bulletin board. In Alicia's hybrid course she always has a welcome announcement that students can see even before the course begins. This announcement, usually posted one week before class starts, offers an inviting way to give students a mini-orientation to the course and sets a precedent for the importance of the bulletin board right away. Alicia includes a little information about her background and interest in the course as well as a heads-up on course materials, texts, and so forth that are needed for the first day. And, of course, the post always ends with a note about how excited she is to meet students on the first day.

Online Lectures

As in face-to-face courses, using a variety of teaching strategies is useful when crafting your online lectures in your interpersonal communication course. Consider incorporating YouTube clips or short popular press articles as "required readings" for the related assignments. Generally, online lectures are much shorter in length than traditional face-to-face classes. Just as long lectures are difficult for maintaining attention in face-to-face classroom formats, extensive lectures are even less effective online. Think about your own Internet use. You likely "Web site-hop" from one page to another, barely spending more than one minute on a page. The same is true for online learners. They have a low threshold for what they can tolerate reading online and can easily experience information overload. Be sure to streamline your information. Alicia recommends you separate the information into "must know" and "nice to know" information when deciding what needs to be put in your lectures. Don't just assume that you can take outlines and lectures from your previous face-to-face courses and simply dump them into the online format.

Depending on how the course is organized, lectures can be video-recorded or audio-recorded in advance or performed "live" online. If you do lecture synchronously, it is still a good idea to record that lecture so students can refer back to it if necessary. Plus, you can save your recorded lecture for future online classes.

Assignments and Activities

There are a variety of ways to assess students' learning in an online interpersonal class through ungraded and graded assignments and activities. The first consideration for designing activities and assignments is to set up your expectations early. This includes information about deadlines, late work deductions (if you accept late work), and how technical difficulties will be handled. Most of this information can be addressed in your Approach to the Course statement discussed earlier. You can easily become overwhelmed with student excuses and questions if you don't have a clear idea of your expectations before posting your assignments.

When determining assignments, activities, quizzes, and exams, also consider the grading aspects of those assessments. Think about your time constraints, the students' workload, and your ability to handle the work. For example, if you assign five discussion posts from each of thirty students, are you going to grade all 150 posts? If not, perhaps you might require fewer posts or you might decide to "spot grade" posts throughout the session. (We discuss grading further in the next section.) In most learning management systems, you can set a deadline for assignments or discussion submissions. If students do not submit by the deadline, the assignment is no longer available for the students to complete.

An example of an online activity to encourage participation comes from one of our teaching assistants. When teaching online, she assigned an interpersonal communication concept to each of her students. The students were required to post a short video (from YouTube or an original recording) that illustrated their assigned concept. The student also had to explain the clip in terms of the concept and pose an open-ended question to the other students on the online discussion board. These were due throughout the semester. The student was graded on the relevancy of the clip, explanation of it in terms of concepts, and on the quality of the discussion question. Other students were then graded on their participation on the discussion board.

Jill Dupy, adjunct instructor at Southern Illinois University Edwardsville and online professor of interpersonal communication at Rasmussen College and McKendree University, suggests that you use media frequently as a learning tool online (personal correspondence, December 13, 2013). She recommends, "Pull in media as much as you can. Students understand the concepts so much better if they can see how they are applied in actual interactions." For example, she uses the film *Waterboy* to demonstrate conflict concepts and the use of exit, voice, loyalty, and neglect. Jill suggests that it is easy to add a variety of clips through YouTube and Hulu, where full or edited versions of television programs, movies, and personal clips are plentiful. We also suggest movieclips.com where you can search for clips from popular movies by title, actor, genre, or even themes like aggression or ethics.

Discussion Boards

Online discussions are often a large component in online classes. As in face-to-face classes, developing useful, effective discussion questions is the key to success. In online discussions, students are more likely to participate than they are in face-to-face classes. Students in online classes tend to answer questions and edit their response more often than students in traditional settings (Karayan & Crowe, 1997). Further, Shuell and Farber (2001) discovered that as students participate more online, their motivation for the course increases.

Following Bloom's taxonomy when developing questions can be useful. These include questions that test the student's knowledge, comprehension, application, analysis, synthesis, and evaluation skills. Sample questions are listed below.

Knowledge — Define "interpersonal communication."
Comprehension — Explain what is meant by psychological noise.
Application — Give an example of a script you follow when ordering food at a restaurant.
Analysis — Compare and contrast I-language with You-language.
Synthesis — Summarize the errors that occur in perception and explain how they can affect your interpersonal communication.
Evaluation — Identify what you believe is the most important concept in the chapter and justify its importance (that is, what makes it the most important concept?).

As you can see, asking questions at the various levels garners very different answers. For example, asking synthesis-type questions is more likely to encourage unique, thoughtful responses as compared to knowledge or comprehension questions.

Some instructors suggest a first deadline for students' initial responses to discussion board prompts and a second deadline for students' comments on others' initial responses. This format alleviates the last-minute flurry of posts and comments and does not punish the students who want to work ahead. Further, utilizing a "practice" discussion board the first week will help students get used to the technology as well as your expectations for their responses. This could even serve as an opportunity for students to introduce themselves to each other. Posting "model" responses in discussion threads would be helpful for students as well. Our colleague Jill Dupy recommends modeling the types of discussion posts that you hope to see from your students (personal correspondence, December 13, 2013). She encourages her students to engage in deeper thinking for the discussion she posts. Jill claims, "Set an example of what you want to see in their posts. Students don't always know how to post. You need to set the standard for them." She also recommends that you encourage frequent interaction with students on the discussion boards and ask for students to participate throughout the week rather than just "dumping" all of their ideas on one day.

We also recommend creating a discussion forum for general questions as well. You should "subscribe" to this forum if possible so you are e-mailed when someone posts a question and, as a result, you can respond to questions in a timely fashion.

As the instructor, you can decide if you want to also participate in discussions, asking further questions or prompting additional reflection. You might also need to refocus or redirect conversations back to your original discussion prompt. At the conclusion of each discussion, it is valuable for you (or a student) to synthesize the discussion, showing connections between the various thoughts or examples and summarizing main ideas. Relatedly, the following week's discussion board could also include a thread in which the students complete this task in addition to that week's discussion prompts. A final suggestion is to have students generate discussion questions as part of a graded assignment. For example, in Alicia's hybrid course she asks each student to sign up for one of the assigned interpersonal course topics at the beginning of the semester. Then, each student is asked to serve as a "discussion facilitator" for that particular topic (e.g., a portion of a chapter for an undergraduate class). The student is then responsible for posting three thought-provoking questions about the topic to generate student participation. The student facilitator must regularly check and respond to students' responses just as an instructor would by commenting and asking follow-up questions. Alicia has found that student facilitators enjoy having the opportunity to guide discussions, while student participants often enjoy responding to the questions their peers ask. Further, student-led questions encourage students to become more engaged in the material and to think more critically about specific topics. And, as an added bonus, instructors may find the student questions are useful for future discussion prompts the next time they teach the course.

Exams

Because it is difficult to ensure that a student taking an online test is not using his or her notes, exams for online classes will likely be in one of two formats: open book or proctored. Asking questions that require students to synthesize or apply information allows you to determine if they learned the material or are simply able to regurgitate information from the textbook or lectures. If using the proctored method, be sure to clearly indicate who qualifies as a proctor and exactly what procedure must be followed before, during, and after the exam.

When designing your exams, use your university resources. After all, your job is to teach the course content; instructional technology's job is to help you and students navigate the technology used for online classes. If your university does not have much support, look at other universities' resources pages, such as:

- University of Illinois' Illinois Online Network: www.ion.uillinois.edu /resources/tutorials/id/index.asp
- West Virginia University eCampus resources: https://ecampus.wvu.edu /faculty/training-and-support
- Missouri State University's Faculty Center for Teaching and Learning: www.missouristate.edu/fctl/

AN ONLINE SYLLABUS

Below you will find Josie's syllabus for her online Interpersonal Communication course at Southern Illinois University Edwardsville.

SPC 103 · INTERPERSONAL COMMUNICATION SKILLS (ONLINE)

Department of Applied Communication Studies

Southern Illinois University Edwardsville

Professor:	Dr. Jocelyn DeGroot	Phone:
Office:	Alumni Hall	E-mail:
Office Hours:	Online Thursdays 1–2 PM (via e-mail or Skype at xxxxx).	
	In addition, I am available by appointment.	

Required Texts

The textbook is required and necessary for successful completion of the course.

McCornack, S. (2010). *Reflect and relate: An introduction to interpersonal communication* (2nd ed.). Boston: Bedford/St. Martin's.

Additional readings will be posted on Blackboard or on e-Reserve as necessary.

Course Description and Objectives

Studying interpersonal communication has a distinct advantage: you are already very experienced at it. Your life is filled with various types of relationships. You spend each day interacting with people at home, at work, in various social settings, and other places. Your past and current relationships as well as your daily interactions with others provide a rich context for analyzing and applying the concepts you will learn in this course. So, reflect on your own experiences and relationships as you engage this course. You will find that such reflection will allow you to better understand your past interpersonal communication experiences and engage your current and future relationships and interactions more knowledgeably.

The purpose of this class is to teach you theories and skills related to successful communication in interpersonal contexts and to discuss vital concepts that are quite simple in theory, but complex in practice. This course is designed to accomplish the following primary objectives:

1. To provide students with a comprehensive knowledge of interpersonal communication theories and processes.
2. To provide students with the ability to apply conceptual ideas about interpersonal communication to practical communication situations.
3. To provide students with the ability to apply key concepts and processes in interpersonal communication.

Specific chapter objectives are provided on Blackboard.

Course Format

This is an online course in which all of the coursework will be completed online and not in the traditional, physical classroom. You are responsible for keeping up with deadlines throughout the semester. Blackboard will be utilized for this course. Grades, supplemental materials, and class announcements will be posted here.

You can download and complete ungraded Reading Notes (available on Blackboard) to help focus your reading of the assigned materials. I will post brief lectures of each chapter to help your understanding of the reading. Reading and lecture quizzes will be completed weekly. Further, you will identify artifacts to illustrate interpersonal concepts and ask relevant critical thinking questions of your classmates on discussion boards. You will then apply what you read and provide real-life examples as you respond to your classmates' critical thinking questions. All assignments are due online through Blackboard. I will post grades on Blackboard within three days of the assignment or exam deadline.

Your SIUE e-mail address will be used for communication purposes. It is your responsibility to check Blackboard and your e-mail regularly. If you have technical difficulties, please contact the help desk at 618-650-5500. They are also available at www.siue.edu/its/bb/. **If you have a technical issue during an assignment submission, it is your responsibility to take a screenshot of the issue and e-mail it to me along with your completed assignment. Computer problems or a poor Internet connection are not excuses for failing to complete your work.**

Turnitin Policy

By taking this course, you agree that all required papers may be subject to submission for textual similarity review to Turnitin for the detection of plagiarism. Some papers submitted for review will be included as source documents in the global Turnitin repository to be used in future reviews. You should remove your name and any other personally identifying information from your papers prior to submission to Turnitin. For additional information on and instructions pertaining to Turnitin, consult the SIUE Turnitin resource page at: www.siue.edu/its /turnitin/.

Course Evaluation

Near the end of this course, you will be asked to complete a departmental course evaluation questionnaire inviting your opinions about the course and the instructor. The Department of Applied Communication Studies and I value your input. The course evaluation will be administered in such a way as to ensure your confidentiality. The teacher will not have access to the information on the evaluation until after grades have been turned in at the end of the semester.

Academic Integrity

University standards regulating academic integrity (e.g., cheating, plagiarism, etc.) are strictly enforced. Plagiarism is a serious offense in this course. Using the words and ideas of others is borrowing something from those individuals. It is always necessary to identify the original source of supporting information; you must cite the source of any material, quoted or paraphrased, used in your presentations. The absence of this documentation constitutes plagiarism — a serious academic and professional offense. Proper documentation requires a bibliography of any outside texts you have consulted, including both traditional sources and online sources. Be careful to document sources within your presentation outline and bibliography as well as orally during any presentations. Merely restating another individual's ideas in different words does not make the ideas yours. Serious infractions of these rules will result in a failing grade in the course. These standards may seem subtle, so feel free to ask if you have questions or concerns. For more information on SIUE's plagiarism policy, visit www.siue.edu/policies/1i6.shtml.

Reasonable Accommodation Policy

Students with disabilities must participate in all programs and activities. Therefore, if you have an identified disability and will need any type of accommodation in this course (e.g., alternate test-taking environment) or have questions about physical access, please inform me as soon as possible. For more information, contact Disability Support Services: http://www.siue.edu/dss/.

Late Work and Incomplete Grade Policy

All assignments, quizzes, and exams must be completed on the date assigned. I WILL NOT accept late work. Be sure to anticipate possible problems that may arise, including computer or Internet problems — begin working on your assignments in advance in order to avoid late-night e-mails to the instructor the night before an assignment is due. In the rare cases where I do allow a make-up assignment, the make-up must be completed by a date and time at my discretion and be accompanied by specific documentation of the absence. In emergencies, I will make other arrangements with individual students, but such cases are relatively rare. I am more understanding if you keep me informed. If you encounter problems, please let me know right away. I may be able to help.

Classroom Civility

Please avoid disruptive behavior that makes it difficult to accomplish our mutual objectives. Avoid inappropriate language and comments on the discussion boards. Please see the University Web site for the SIUE Student Conduct Code (www.siue.edu/policies/3c1.shtml).

ASSIGNMENTS

[Note: See Course Packet on Blackboard for specific assignment requirements.]

Course Format and Syllabus Quiz (5 points each)

On the first day of the semester, you will take an online quiz on the syllabus and format of the course. This is meant to help you get acquainted with the course policies and format of the course. You will have 30 minutes to take the quiz once you begin.

Weekly Quizzes (14 @ 5 points each)

Each week, you will take an online reading quiz on the chapter(s) covered that week. The quizzes will open on Tuesday at 8 AM and close Wednesday at 8 PM. You will have 10 minutes to take the quiz once you begin.

Artifact Discussion (25 Points)

You will sign up for one topic on the syllabus (link to signup will be provided on Blackboard). Using that week's readings as a basis, you will find an artifact (video, song, lyrics, news article) that relates to the information of that day. In your posting, you will use course concepts and vocabulary to clearly explain how that artifact is linked to the day's reading(s). By Tuesday at 8 AM, you will post this artifact, your explanation, and a relevant discussion question to the appropriate discussion thread on Blackboard for others to discuss. This should be an open-ended question that stimulates critical thinking. You are graded on your artifact, explanation of the artifact, and the question posed. An example is available on Blackboard.

Artifact Response (10 @ 5 Points)

You will respond to at least 10 Artifact Discussions posted by your classmates (you cannot respond to your own). You will watch, read, or listen to the artifact posted by your classmate and answer the question posed. Provide specific, concrete examples in your responses in addition to course vocabulary/terminology as appropriate. Deadlines are indicated on the discussion thread itself and are generally 3 days after the initial artifact is posted.

Exams (2 @ 50 points)

Exams will assess your understanding of interpersonal communication concepts and theories, as well as your application and integration abilities. The exams will consist of multiple-choice and short-answer questions. Exams are open book/open notes and will be taken on Blackboard. The link will become live for the designated time period. You will have 1 hour to take the test once you begin. There is a midterm examination and a non-comprehensive final examination. Each exam is worth 50 points.

Course Assignments and Grades

Syllabus Quiz	(5 points)	5
Reading Quizzes	(14 x 5 points)	70
Artifact Discussion	(25 points)	25
Artifact Response	(10 x 5 points)	50
Exams	(2 x 50 points)	100
Total		**250 points**

There are **250** total points in the class. You can determine your percentage (and grade) by totaling the points you have accumulated and dividing those points by the number of points possible to date.

    The following grading scale will be used in the course:

A = 90%–100%	(225 – 250 pts)
B = 80%–89.9%	(200 – 224 pts)
C = 70%–79.9%	(175 – 199 pts)
D = 60%–69.9%	(150 – 174 pts)
F = below 59.9%	**(149 pts and below)**

Tentative Schedule (subject to change)

WEEK	TOPIC	ASSIGNMENT
1	Introduction to Course	
	PART ONE: Your Part of an Interpersonal Exchange	
	Introducing Interpersonal Communication: The Basics	Chapter 1
2	Considering Self	Chapter 2
3	Perceiving Others	Chapter 3
4	Experiencing and Expressing Emotions	Chapter 4
	Developing Interpersonal Competence	Chapter 8
5	Listening Actively	Chapter 5
6	Communicating Verbally	Chapter 6
7	Communicating Nonverbally	Chapter 7
8	**Midterm Exam** **Available 12 Noon – 6 PM**	**Midterm Exam** **Chapters 1-8**
	PART TWO: Interpersonal Relationships	
9	Managing Conflict and Power	Chapter 9
10	Romantic Relationships	Chapter 10; pp. 320–348
11	The Dark Side of Romantic Relationships	Chapter 10; pp. 349–359
12	Long-Distance Relationships and Online Communication	Article on Blackboard
13	Relationships with Family	Chapter 11; pp. 363–381
14	Relationships with Friends	Chapter 11; pp. 381–397
15	Relationships in the Workplace	Chapter 12
Finals	**Final Exam** **Available 12 Noon – 6 PM**	**Final Exam** **Chapters 9-12; Bb article**

GRADING INTERPERSONAL COMMUNICATION ONLINE

When grading assignments submitted in online classes, it can be useful to provide more written feedback than you would in a FTF course. Various software programs (such as Turnitin with grademark or Microsoft Word's track changes option) allow you to make comments right in the student's paper. This allows the student to see exactly where they lost points and determine how they can improve for the next assignment. It also cuts down on student e-mails to you asking why they lost points. For example, to prevent some of these problems and general confusion over grading, Josie provides feedback on items that she thinks her students would ask about. In addition, you might choose to compile a list of the most commonly made student mistakes and discuss them in an online lecture. This shows the students that you are reading all of their work and are acknowledging difficulties they might be having as a group.

Developing Course Packets

As in face-to-face courses, rubrics or assessment sheets are useful in online classes so students know in advance how they will be graded. Both Alicia and Josie create and upload course packets for all of their classes. These packets contain assignment descriptions and assessment sheets or rubrics for each assignment in the course. The packet provides more specific information than the syllabus and offers details such as requirements for page limits, time limits, number of sources required, style for citations, and so forth. It can offer extra guidance such as recommendations for a successful "A" assignment, tips on finding scholarly sources, writing suggestions, APA guidelines, etc. A thorough course packet can help encourage students to keep up with the requirements for the course rather than having you constantly serving as their "taskmaster." Students appreciate having the detailed information about each assignment right at their fingertips whenever they are working on an assignment. The packet can also help the students decide if the course load is manageable for them before staying enrolled in the course for the semester.

Consistency in Grading

Again, because online communication is more text-based than face-to-face communication is, comments are vital. Therefore, when grading, it is useful to provide as much feedback as possible so the students understand where they lost points and what they did well. Be sure to grade several students' work in one session to ensure you are applying your standards equally across students' work. When possible, grade within your learning management system so assignment grades are automatically entered into your gradebook. Finally, be consistent in terms of when grades are posted. At the beginning of the term, you should tell students when they can expect their grades to be available. For example, maybe you will post all grades from the previous week on Wednesday. This helps set the expectation for grades and can alleviate some of your students' anxiety about their performance in the class. A colleague who frequently teaches courses at a completely online university suggested that students often judge their instructor's effectiveness by their grading consistency and timeliness. She said students quickly label you as the "teacher that never returns grades" or the "good one" who quickly posts grades and provides clear feedback.

CHALLENGES OF TEACHING ONLINE

While teaching an online interpersonal communication class can be rewarding and interesting, it certainly is not without challenges. A common complaint that we hear from our colleagues teaching online classes is that students often have excuses about why they didn't turn in their assignments. Sounds similar to your traditional face-to-face classes, right? However, the added challenge in online classes is that students frequently add technical challenges to their lists of problems through excuses such as "my computer doesn't work," "my Internet was out all day," and "I sent this at X time and I don't know why you didn't get it."

As indicated earlier, plan ahead for technical issues. We suggest requiring students to e-mail a screen shot of any error message experienced during assignment submission in addition to their assignment content. Some students experience technical problems related to the ability of their computers or Internet. Bandwidth and software issues are the most common. Some Information Technologies departments provide students with the minimum requirements necessary to successfully participate in online courses. Check with your IT department to see if this information is available to you and your students.

Cheating is an issue for all teachers, regardless of course format. When giving exams, we recommend using one of the methods discussed earlier in the chapter. Turnitin is a good resource to utilize if your school supports it. Students submit their papers to Turnitin.com (supported through Blackboard). The Web site then compares their writing to other student papers in the repository as well as Internet sources to determine the originality of the student's writing. You can then view the originality report and determine if similar passages are plagiarized.

Students sometimes think online courses should be easier than face-to-face courses. As discussed earlier, this is not often the case. Rather, online courses often allow for more flexibility with regard to time, but more of a time commitment overall. Some students are not aware of, or prepared for, the huge time commitment required from an online course. This is why it is important to provide them with information about the time requirements, assignments, and necessary participation in advance so they can determine if the online format is right for them. Another suggestion is to encourage students to take a self-evaluation to determine their readiness for an online course. The University of Illinois has one at: www.ion.uillinois.edu/resources/tutorials/pedagogy/selfEval.asp.

Copyright Information

When posting readings for students online, it is important to check with your library (or relevant university office) to determine that you follow any applicable copyright laws. This can be a complicated, messy area, and how copyrights are handled varies from college to college. At SIUE, teachers send the source and source information to a specialist in our library who acquires copyright permission to use a particular reading. Your institution's guidelines on what is considered fair use or open-access can depend a lot on the preferences of their legal team. It is always best to check before posting items that could fall under copyright protection.

GUIDELINES FOR TEACHING ONLINE

Although early researchers doubted the ability of computers to allow people to develop relationships in an online context, Walther's (1992) Social Information Processing (SIP) Theory indicates that online communication *can* aid in relationship development and maintenance. SIP theory indicates that online communicators are able to adapt to using the computer for communication and use it to develop close relationships, but it takes longer than it would if the two communicators were talking face-to-face. In fact, Walther (1996) later discussed and argued that, due to characteristics of computer-mediated communication (like online disinhibition discussed earlier), relationships can actually become hyperpersonal, or even more intimate than they would have become in face-to-face contexts.

What this means for you is that your online class will likely not "jell" as quickly as your face-to-face classes usually do. You can help this process along by assigning activities (some of which are discussed earlier in the chapter) in which the students must interact with each other and with you (on- or offline). These kinds of assignments will also help develop your online social presence. Social presence is the degree of interpersonal contact (Gunawardena & Zittle, 1997) and is related to immediacy. In a face-to-face classroom, instructors gesture, smile, use humor, and address students by name to establish immediacy and social presence (Christophel, 1990). Social presence is just as important to establish in the online classroom. Richardson and Swan (2003) found that when students have high perceptions of online presence, they also had positive perceptions of perceived learning and satisfaction with their instructor. They also found that, specifically, class discussions and group projects were related to higher social presence scores.

To help establish a sense of community or cohesiveness among students, we suggest requiring students to create an introduction video or personal profile within the learning management system. You will also want to establish your own presence as the instructor. You can achieve this by posting your own personal video that introduces you to the students and gives an overview of the course. You might also consider holding office hours via video chat, as discussed earlier in the chapter. If you choose to utilize online discussion boards, make your presence known there as well. Comment on students' input and ask questions — not as a teacher, but as a participant on the board.

Kristin Ruppert-Leach, Assistant Professor of Applied Communication Studies at Southwestern Illinois College, has taught and developed interpersonal communication courses for five different community colleges and online programs, and she suggests that an online presence is essential in teaching any online course:

> Be present in your course. You can do this in a number of ways. The most primary way you can be present in an interpersonal course is via the discussion board. Make sure you post as much as possible and encourage discussion as much as possible.[3]

Self-disclosure can also help develop your online presence. As discussed earlier, online disinhibition allows for increased self-disclosure, which can have a positive or a negative effect (Suler, 2004). While you might feel more free to reveal information about yourself, remember to consider if you would reveal that information in a traditional face-to-face classroom before hitting the "send" or "submit" button — and encourage your students to do the same.

If you are looking for additional resources or advice for teaching online, check out some of our favorite sources:

1. Illinois Online Network Online Teaching Activity Index. www.ion .uillinois.edu/resources/otai/
   This webpage contains a variety of online teaching activities that can be adapted for your own classroom use.
2. Ko, S., & Rossen, S. (2010). *Teaching online: A practical guide*. New York: Routledge.
   This book offers several practical tips for teaching any online course.
3. Michigan State University Office of Faculty & Organizational Development. http://fod.msu.edu/oir/online-teaching
   This is Michigan State University's collection of resources for online teaching. The page includes information about teaching hybrid and online classes. It also lists Web pages with additional online teaching resources.
4. Minnesota State Colleges & Universities Resources for Teaching Online. http://asa.mnscu.edu/facultydevelopment/online-teaching/
   The MnSCU Web page has a variety of resources for online instruction, including Desire2Learn (D2L), distance learning, e-Learning, and online teaching.
5. Phipps, J. J. (2005). E-Journaling: Achieving interactive education online. *Educause Quarterly*, 28(1): 62–65, from www.educause.edu/ir/library/pdf /EQM0519.pdf
   This article highlights the importance of using journals in online classes and offers some great suggestions for how to include journaling in your online course.

---

[3]Personal correspondence with Alicia Alexander, December 13, 2013.

CONCLUSION

In this chapter we covered the many benefits of teaching an online interpersonal communication course; the differences between hybrid, online, and face-to-face interpersonal courses; strategies for engaging online learners; suggestions for course development, organization, and grading; as well as ways for overcoming challenges of teaching interpersonal communication online. If you are new to online courses, still considering trying one, or revamping your existing online course, we hope we have inspired you to take on the challenge of trying your interpersonal course in a new format. We trust you will find online courses can be just as rewarding and engaging as your traditional face-to-face course. Good luck, and we wish you the best in your online adventures!

CHAPTER

7

Foundational Resources

In this chapter we will concentrate on technical aspects of locating and reading materials that support an entry-level course in interpersonal communication. You will find an introductory discussion on types of sources and how to read them efficiently, advice on building a personal library, and an annotated bibliography of eighty-five citations. This chapter will help increase your teaching effectiveness by showing you how to use foundational resources in an informed and systematic manner. Let's begin by looking at the types of resources available.

PRIMARY AND SECONDARY RESOURCES

Teachers need both primary and secondary sources to understand the scope of the field. Primary sources are the original findings reported by the authors and/ or researchers themselves. This primary source material constitutes our teaching foundation and is the initial word on the theory or concept in question. It is best to go to the original source whenever possible so that we can read for ourselves the researchers' principal ideas. In general, it is recommended that we read the research in the language of its time and in the source in which it was originally published because once a primary source is interpreted and printed somewhere else, ideas can change or become distorted. For example, Erving Goffman's *The Presentation of Self in Everyday Life* was published in 1959, yet we are still using many of his ideas about impression management and interpersonal persuasion. The phrase *impression management* wasn't used 45 years ago, so it is a good idea to read the original to get the holistic feel and understanding of his ideas. Also, the language and examples he uses are somewhat different from what an author might use today, so reading the original may help you recognize any distortions that could occur as contemporary authors invoke Goffman's book. Reading the original source makes you a more grounded reader intellectually and historically.

Secondary sources, such as textbooks, are valuable because they show us how our colleagues interpret knowledge. We need to see how others frame and interpret the scholarship of interpersonal communication because that is an indicator of how the material is valued and presented to students. Just looking at a textbook for its point of view, what is included and excluded, and how the material is organized tells a teacher a great deal about how the principles of interpersonal communication are taught. A secondary source is often a shortcut because someone else does the thinking for you. If you are short on time, this could be a quick answer to your need for knowledge. However, reading primary sources is the only way to fully ground yourself in original ideas. As a teacher, you need to make decisions about how central a role secondary sources will play in your teaching.

Consider the following instructive activity. Compare five interpersonal communication textbooks on the following points: overall organization, major themes, and main topic covered in each chapter. Where do these textbooks converge and diverge? What does this tell you about the general way instructors view the appropriate teaching of interpersonal communication? Do you agree or disagree with the general approach you see in these textbooks? How does an activity like this help you think about your teaching and resource selection?

Types of Primary and Secondary Sources

Primary and secondary sources come in various formats; following is a guide to help you identify the sources that may be found in the annotated bibliography at the end of this chapter. Note that different formats have unique structural features that determine how a reader should approach the material; we will point out those features. Types of sources you may read include the following.

Edited Anthology.   This is a collection of essays or chapters by different authors that targets various aspects of the same general topic. Anthologies can be a collection of research reports, factual essays, historical pieces, critical articles, or a combination of these. One of the best ways to determine the structure of an anthology is to read the editor's preface or introduction. Then study the table of contents to see how the articles relate to the central theme of the anthology.

Both Sage and Lawrence Erlbaum publishers are known for their excellent research anthologies on interpersonal communication topics. These anthologies typically comprise a combination of literature reviews, theoretical suggestions, and research reports. An anthology such as this would be considered primary because the research is original and the content theorizing. For example, the annotated bibliography, the *Handbook of Communication and Social Interaction Skills* (2003), edited by John Greene and Brant Burleson, is a collection of literature reviews on a range of interpersonal contexts connected to competence. It is a research-based anthology that goes beyond what a textbook is designed to do and includes contributions from experts in the field.

Journal Articles.   In the social sciences, journal articles are usually professional reports of scientific studies and are considered primary sources. These articles report research findings about human behavior, helping us to understand its patterns and the way research supports theories about human behavior. Great journals for interpersonal communication include *Personal Relationships, Journal of Social and Personal Relationships*, and *Journal of Family Communication*. This type of text is best understood if you have a command of both scientific methods for conducting research and the typical vocabulary or jargon for that topic area. If you do not have knowledge of scientific research methods, do not be deterred.

The article title reveals the main concept or theoretical area under investigation. If there is an abstract available, read it to get the summary and basic findings of the study. The body of most social science reports is divided into four parts: introduction, methods and procedures, results, and discussion and conclusions. The methods and procedures section will be the most technical, so if you don't have the background for it, you might want to concentrate more on the other three sections. There are valuable ideas to explore in all of the sections, but the discussion and conclusions will usually summarize the study for you.

Book.   This type of source is a report of an entire theory, in most instances. A book is usually the culmination of many years of research wherein the author collects and presents his or her research findings into a coherent whole, rather than as a collection of piecemeal journal articles published over the testing of a theory. Books frequently include chapters on the theoretical framework, the instrumentation used to collect data, a review of the studies done over a period of time, the propositions and models that are the core of the theory, and some criticism of the theory. These books are valuable for the extended knowledge provided.

For example, Irwin Altman and Dalmas Taylor's book *Social Penetration: The Development of Interpersonal Relationships* (1973/1983) presents the theory of social penetration. Many interpersonal communication textbooks present the famous "onion model" from social penetration theory, but it's not until you read the primary source that you understand in depth what the model means. Reading the original source can help you clarify the model in the textbook and can help you teach it in a way that students can understand it is more than just a tool for understanding self-disclosure in relationship development. Students may also find that "popular press" texts written on various interpersonal communication topics are useful as well. For example, students often like to refer to Dr. Phil McGraw's books or Dr. John Gray's books such as *Men Are from Mars, Women Are from Venus*. While these books can be useful for some insight on the topic, be sure to encourage them to find more academic sources on the subject for class research.

Traditional Textbook.   As was stated earlier, a traditional textbook is a secondary source. This type of source is often easy to read because the author uses many pedagogical tools (headings, boxes, discussion questions, a glossary, bold type, and exercises) to help you understand the content of the text. The annotated bibliography at the end of this chapter lists a few textbooks, which have been included either because they are considered classics in the field, such as Miller and Steinberg's *Between People* (1975), or because they are an extension of an author's original theorizing on an interpersonal communication topic, such as *Competent Communication* (1997) by O'Hair, Friedrich, Wiemann, and Wiemann. Such cases reveal some crossover between primary and secondary reporting of knowledge.

BUILDING A PERSONAL LIBRARY

In order to maintain your theoretical knowledge, you should build a basic library of sources for yourself as you can afford to do so. Start with collecting items that you use frequently in the classroom; it can be disconcerting not to own materials that you need. There are three avenues you can take to build a personal collection of resources: First, photocopy or download journal articles (using tools such as Journal Finder from your campus library connection) and slip those into a file folder. Put in one item per file folder, label the folder, and file alphabetically by author last name. This will be your vertical, or hanging, file. If you subscribe to a number of journals, mark potential articles with Post-it notes so you can access them quickly.

Second, pay attention to the publishers' catalogues that come in the mail, and carefully scrutinize the interpersonal communication offerings to learn trends and determine what materials may be offered as courtesy items. Do not abuse this privilege! Order desk copies only for those items that you plan to consider for use. Also make a point of ordering library copies so that when you mention these sources in class, students can go and have a look for themselves. We advise against the habit of loaning your own materials. Our experience is that personal materials often don't come back, or they are in worse shape than when you loaned them. We also find that we never know when we might need a resource from our own library. If it's loaned out, we don't have it to do our job. It may sound harsh not to loan to others, but the reality is that books and other materials are precious commodities that help you with your work. Protect them.

The third avenue for acquisition of materials is to buy books as you need to, or as you come across out-of-print items in used bookstores. (Amazon.com is not always the answer to your quest!) Keep in your wallet the titles of the top five out-of-print books on your wish list so that you can buy them when you find them. You may also want to spend more time at exhibitors' booths when attending conventions—that way you can actually look at books you are thinking of purchasing for your own library. There is usually a convention discount offered as well.

Why spend time reading and collecting a library? It is our professional obligation to stay current in the field. The one complaint we always had as students was when we took a class for which the professor had not updated the course readings in a decade! We vowed never to be one of those professors, and writing this chapter reinforces for us the need to be systematic in keeping a collection of materials up-to-date and, subsequently, the materials used in class up-to-date as well.

ANNOTATED BIBLIOGRAPHY

The following annotated bibliography lists eighty-five sources that will ground your knowledge in interpersonal communication and assist with teaching an introductory course in interpersonal communication. The bibliography is a compilation of both historic works and current resources and, although it consists primarily of books, lists some journal articles as well. Most of the publishers in the bibliography have specialties. For example, Sage Publications is known for up-to-date research anthologies. Knowing who publishes what may help you make decisions about which catalogues to keep up with and whose exhibition booth to attend when you are at a conference. Of course, you cannot teach without watching films, reading novels, and perusing Web sites, among the many sources of information available on personal relationships. However, the purpose here is to provide an academic grounding in the scholarship of interpersonal communication.

The bibliography has been constructed to provide you with more information than is normally found in a citation. You will note that there are four primary fields from which we draw knowledge in interpersonal communication: communication, sociology, anthropology, and psychology. Within psychology we are informed by cognitive, social, and clinical approaches. We include social science (empirical) and interpretive work to demonstrate the range of theory that underlies interpersonal communication. Even though many teachers find it easy to use a skills-based, or empirical, approach to teaching a basic undergraduate course, we cannot emphasize enough that philosophy, interpretation, and behavior all play important roles in our teaching and practice of interpersonal communication.

There are few journal articles in the bibliography for a reason. The sheer quantity of available journal articles makes it almost impossible to select something definitive. Instead, we have selected classic articles (e.g., Berger & Calabrese, 1975; Burgoon & Hale, 1988; Gibb, 1961; Knapp, Hart, & Dennis, 1974) to show you the beginnings of important concepts and theories and to remind you that it is pedagogically sound to cite research findings in class (e.g., Owen, 1984; Planalp & Honeycutt, 1985). Students do want to know "what the research says," and journal articles allow you to see the details of the communication process under study. As a professional, you should read regional (e.g., *Communication Quarterly*) and national (e.g., *Communication Monographs, Human Communication Research*) journals on a regular basis, but it is also helpful to read the interdisciplinary journals that pertain specifically to interpersonal communication, such as *Journal of Social and Personal Relationships* and *Personal Relationships*.

There are two ways you can use the annotated bibliography: as an alphabetical list by author, or as a guide to specific topic areas. In the table below you will find an alphabetical list of topic areas in the first column and a suggested set of sources by their number for those topics in the second column.

If you are interested in:	See items numbered:
Apprehension (Shyness, Reticence)	22, 40
Attachment	6
Attraction	11, 21, 36, 68
Attribution	16, 36, 61, 81
Communication Climate	8, 18, 21, 30
Competence	8, 21, 33, 40, 53, 64, 69

(Continued)

If you are interested in:	See items numbered:
Compliance Gaining	28, 48
Computer-Mediated Communication	5, 72, 78, 79
Conflict Management	26, 27, 28, 29, 37, 39, 47, 49, 60, 72, 78, 79, 82
Constructivism	23
Conversation	14, 52, 67
Culture	51, 54, 56, 63, 84, 85
Dark Side	20, 21, 37, 83
Deception	14, 20, 43
Dialectics	8, 47, 55, 58
Dialogue	8, 39, 67
Difficulty, Difficult People	26, 32, 40, 41, 65
Discourse (Conversation) Analysis	52
Divorce	1, 27
Empathy	13, 49, 59
Expectancies	15, 16, 68
Face, Facework, Face Negotiation	19, 25, 32
Family	1, 27, 29, 33, 37, 40, 55, 65, 75
Friendship	25, 33, 37, 54, 58, 61, 83
Gender, Sex Differences, Sexual Orientation	3, 24, 25, 35, 37, 40, 56, 62, 83, 85
Humanistic Philosophy	13, 38, 59
Impression Formation and Management (See also Facework)	5, 31, 33, 61
Intercultural Communication	34, 47
Johari Window	46
Journal Articles	4, 9, 15, 30, 43, 48, 56, 57, 62, 70, 72, 78, 79
Listening	12
Love and Romance	24, 37, 44, 61, 71, 85
Marriage	28, 54, 85
Metacommunication	63, 80
Miscommunication	46, 50
Nonverbal Communication	14, 15, 34, 47
Paradox (Double Binds)	20, 80
Pedagogy	17, 76
Power	28, 29, 48, 53, 82
Prejudice and Racism	37, 74
Relational Culture	84
Relational Structure	8, 28, 80, 84
Relational Theories	2, 9, 23, 26, 36, 53, 63, 66, 73, 76, 80
Relationship Development, Maintenance, Dissolution (Stage Theory)	2, 4, 27, 41, 60, 61, 70

(Continued)

If you are interested in:	See items numbered:
Research Anthologies	20, 22, 24, 25, 27, 33, 35, 37, 42, 55, 61, 85
Roles	5, 10
Rules	23, 56, 65, 84
Self-Awareness	13, 46, 59
Self-Disclosure	2, 25, 38, 46, 49, 55, 60, 62
Social Cognition	9, 16, 42, 49, 57, 61, 81
Social Construction (Interpretive Approach)	10, 39, 45, 54, 64, 67
Social Exchange and Equity	60, 73, 77
Speech Accommodation	61
Stalking	21, 25
Stigma	32
Symbolic Interaction	10, 28, 64
Systems Theory	7, 29, 63
Textbooks	3, 5, 12, 14, 23, 29, 39, 41, 47, 49, 53, 76, 81, 82, 83, 84
Uncertainty Reduction	9, 57

1 Afifi, T. D., & Schrodt, P. (2003). "Feeling caught" as a mediator of adolescents' and young adults' avoidance and satisfaction with their parents in divorced and non-divorced households. *Communication Monographs, 70,* 142–173.
Communication
This frequently cited article on family relationships examines the extent to which young adults "feel caught" between their parents when dealing with divorce. This study suggests that parents' demand-withdraw patterns and communication competence have a strong impact on their children. Further, findings revealed that children of divorce experience greater avoidance and less satisfaction and less closeness than do children from first-marriage families.

2 Altman, I., & Taylor, D. A. (1983). *Social penetration: The development of interpersonal relationships.* New York, NY: Irvington Publishers. (Original work published 1973)
HM132.A38 1983 Psychology
One of the early conceptualizations of relational stages, social penetration theory examines dyads in light of growth and deterioration, breadth and depth of intimacy, personality, and costs and rewards. This is the source of the famous "onion model" that is often mistaken as a model of self-disclosure. Rather, what is described is a range of verbal and nonverbal communication behaviors that assist in social bonding.

3 Backlund, P. M., & Williams, M. R. (Eds.). (2004). *Readings in gender communication.* Belmont, CA: Thomson/Wadsworth.
P96.S48 R430 2004 Communication, Interdisciplinary

This "edgy" anthology of thirty-one readings is written by both scholars and students, and the essays include research reports, stories, personal experiences, and interpretive analyses of a wide range of communication concepts. More practical than theoretical, the book will jump-start numerous class discussions on topics such as tattoos, cyberspace, urban music, clothes, and the many facets of gender manifestations in personal relationships.

4 Banks, S. P., Altendorf, D. M., Greene, J. O., & Cody, M. J. (1987). An examination of relationship disengagement: Perceptions, breakup strategies and outcomes. *The Western Journal of Speech Communication, 51*, 19–41.
PN4071.W75 Communication
Using a questionnaire to probe the relational disengagement behavior of 310 respondents, the researchers shed further light on earlier studies done by Baxter and Cody. The report is a practical look at the five strategies of disengagement: justification, avoidance, negative identity management, de-escalation, and positive tone. Results indicate that partners who wish to disengage do consider costs, intimacy, network influences, and quality of the dyad when selecting strategies.

5 Barnes, S. B. (2003). Internet interpersonal relationships. In *Computer-mediated communication: Human-to-human communication across the Internet* (pp. 136–159). Boston, MA: Allyn and Bacon.
HM851.B37 2002 Communication
This chapter demonstrates how interpersonal concepts are manifested on the Internet. Barnes examines motives for interacting online, types of Internet relationships, and relationship development. Relational structure, social exchange-reciprocity, language, social presence, roles, and impression management are all addressed. This informative essay takes the communication process into a medium that is fast becoming a preferred way for students to relate interpersonally.

6 Bartholomew, K. (1990). Avoidance of intimacy: An attachment perspective. *Journal of Social and Personal Relationships, 7*, 147–178.
Psychology
This article articulates the importance of attachment theory and the implications of attachment and fear of intimacy in adult relationships. Bartholomew discovered the four-group model of attachment styles in adults including two types of fearful and two types of dismissive. The emotional and interpersonal consequences of the two styles are discussed.

7 Bateson, G. (1972). *Steps to an ecology of mind*. New York, NY: Ballantine.
GN6.B3 1972 Anthropology, Interdisciplinary
In this collection of three dozen essays and lectures written over thirty-five years, Bateson presents an accumulation of ideas he calls "minds." The broad range of ideas interacting in each essay requires the reader to know about anthropology, evolution, culture, psychiatry, theories of knowledge, and a systems-cybernetics perspective. His goal is to demonstrate an integrated set of ideas that create a literal mindset that he compares to how

we understand eco-systems. Part III is most beneficial to communication instructors because it discusses relationships, double binds, and cybernetics.

8 Baxter, L. A., & Montgomery, B. M. (1996). *Relating: Dialogues and dialectics.* New York, NY: Guilford.
P94.7 B39 1996 Communication
Relating provides both historical and theoretical background to the relational dialectics perspective. The authors compile a comprehensive review of their and others' research over ten chapters. Included are discussions on assumptions, history, rethinking aspects of interpersonal communication, dialogue, and competence. The thirty-page reference list is a helpful resource for further study.

9 Berger, C. R., & Calabrese, R. J. (1975). Some explorations in initial interaction and beyond: Toward a theory of interpersonal communication. *Human Communication Research, 1,* 99–112.
P91.3H85 Communication
This original essay launched a forty-year research agenda to build and test uncertainty reduction theory. Initially proposing a developmental theory of interpersonal communication, Berger and Calabrese offer a theoretical model of seven axioms and twenty-one theorems to explain what happens communicatively when people first meet and attempt to develop a relationship. The fundamental concept of uncertainty reduction remains a staple in the interpersonal communication course.

10 Berger, P. L., & Luckmann, T. (1966). *The social construction of reality: A treatise in the sociology of knowledge.* New York, NY: Anchor Books.
BD175.B4 1989 Sociology
The original source for the interpretive perspective on interpersonal communication process, this book fully explains the claim that "reality is socially constructed." Part I establishes everyday life as a product of social interaction and language, where communication maintains reality. Part II, on objective reality, examines how institutions help organize and control people through work and roles. Part III, on subjective reality, is a symbolic interaction look at how the self gets socialized through interaction with significant others and institutions.

11 Berscheid, E., & Reis, H. T. (1998). Attraction and close relationships. In D. T. Gilbert, S. T. Fiske, & G. Lindzey (Eds.), *The handbook of social psychology, Vol. II* (4th ed., pp. 193–281). Boston, MA: McGraw-Hill.
HM251.H224 1998 v. 2 Social Psychology
This chapter provides a comprehensive overview of attraction theory. Shifting from attraction in first encounters to acknowledging attraction in ongoing relationships, the review chronologically tracks the development of attraction as the concept functions throughout the life of a relationship. The authors situate the chapter empirically and then chronologically discuss the attraction literature in the field of social psychological theory. Looking at research as it has developed over time allows the reader to see

that we have broadened our understanding of the concept from something that helps relationships to develop initially to the role attraction plays in partners' perceptions of ongoing satisfaction in a dyad. There is a wealth of information here that will assist in classroom discussion on this important topic.

12 Brownell, J. (2006). *Listening: Attitudes, principles, and skills* (3rd ed.). Boston, MA: Pearson/Allyn and Bacon.
BF323.L5 B663 2006 Communication
Using a behavioral approach to improve listening skills, the book is framed around the HURIER model: hearing, understanding, remembering, interpreting, evaluating, and responding. This model is useful for a skills-based course, and the book provides many case studies and ideas for application. Even though the book is based on a relational perspective, the chapter on types of listening relationships demonstrates that the HURIER model needs appropriate application to work effectively.

13 Buber, M. (1970). *I and thou* (Walter Kaufmann, trans.). New York, NY: Charles Scribner's Sons. (Original work published 1937)
B3213.B83 I213 1970 Theology, Philosophy
You do not need a background in religion or philosophy to understand the compassion for humanity or the concern for the loss of interpersonal connection that is the focus of Buber's classic treatise. Walter Kaufmann's translation, together with an extended prologue, is considered the definitive clarification on Buber's first (1923) and second (1957) editions of *I and Thou*. The book is divided into three parts: Part One looks at "I"; Part Two looks at the impersonal world of "it"; Part Three examines "you" as the spiritual connection of people through God. Buber argues that the I–You relationship accounts for the most valid understanding of a true interpersonal relationship because people are connected through each other and in the context of spirituality. He calls this "authentic interpersonalness."

14 Burgoon, J., Buller, D. B., & Woodall, W. G. (1989). *Nonverbal communication: The unspoken dialogue.* New York, NY: Harper & Row.
BF637.N66.B87 1989 Communication
This popular nonverbal communication textbook offers a more in-depth look at nonverbal codes and their function in relational communication. In addition to chapters on kinesics, proxemics, the environment, appearance, and so forth, the second half of the book puts these codes into play in relational processes such as conversation, deception, and the expression of emotion.

15 Burgoon, J. K., & Hale, J. L. (1988). Nonverbal expectancy violations: Model elaboration and application to immediacy behaviors. *Communication Monographs, 55,* 58–79.
PN4077.S6 Communication

Although Expectancy Violations Theory (EVT) has been refined and extended for more than twenty-five years, this article outlines the fundamental concepts and propositions that are the foundation of the theory. The article also includes an empirical study that tests EVT for application to friendship and immediacy. The visual model presented is helpful, as are the explanations of its components: expectancies, violations and arousal, communicator reward valence, behavior interpretation and evaluation, and violation valence.

16 Canary, D. J., Cody, M. J., & Manusov, V. L. (2003). Four important cognitive processes. In K. M. Galvin & P. J. Cooper (Eds.), *Making connections: Readings in relational communication* (pp. 42–51). Los Angeles, CA: Roxbury Publishing.
BF637.C45 M33 2003 Communication
This book is a collection of reprints on many basic interpersonal topics. The chapter by Canary and his colleagues summarizes crucial cognitive processes that most teachers address in interpersonal communication courses: interpersonal expectancies, attributions, person perception, and stereotypes. The resources at the end of the chapter provide suggestions for more in-depth reading in social cognition.

17 Cooper, P. J., & Simonds, C. J. (2003). *Communication for the classroom teacher* (7th ed.). Boston. MA: Allyn and Bacon.
LB1033.C64 2003 Communication, Pedagogy
Although this book is aimed at students training to be communication teachers, there are a number of valuable charts and references to help any teacher improve his or her knowledge and practice of teaching. Because the authors are communication professors themselves, the perspective on teaching is one where the teacher-student relationship is seen as interpersonal. This book is a good motivator for practicing the kinds of skills we are teaching our students to master: listening, discussing, information sharing, and influencing.

18 Cupach, W. R., & Canary, D. J. (2000). *Competence in interpersonal conflict.* Prospect Heights, IL: Waveland.
Communication
This book explores the intersection between ethics and the process of interpersonal conflict. Cupach and Canary begin to outline a competence-based model that guides the interpersonal conflict process. This model accounts for the needs and wants of both disputants with the goal of finding common ground and meeting both people's expectations.

19 Cupach, W. R., & Metts, S. (1994). *Facework.* Thousand Oaks, CA: Sage.
HM132.C86 1994 Communication
This book in the Sage Series on Close Relationships is a heuristic explication of face management theory that brings Goffman's (1967) original work

into the field of communication. The authors argue that face is a salient issue in all interaction, but particularly in difficult interaction such as embarrassing situations and relationship dissolution. They examine gaining, maintaining, and losing face. Managing face constitutes a feature of competent interaction and is a skill for students to learn.

20 Cupach, W. R., & Spitzberg, B. H. (Eds.). (1994). *The dark side of interpersonal communication.* Hillsdale, NJ: Erlbaum.
BF637.C45.D335 1994 Communication
One of the first to focus on negative aspects of interpersonal interaction, this book has spawned much research since its publication. Thirteen chapters explore a range of understudied topics that balance our focus on positive aspects of relating. Such topics include incompetence, paradoxes, deception, relational transgression, privacy invasion, and abuse.

21 Cupach, W. R., & Spitzberg, B. H. (2004). *The dark side of relationship pursuit: From attraction to obsession and stalking.* Mahwah, NJ: Erlbaum.
HM1106.C86 2004 Communication
Continuing their interest in negative aspects of relating, Cupach and Spitzberg here focus on stalking, something many students have experienced. This book synthesizes the interdisciplinary research on obsessive relational intrusion (ORI) and stalking and theorizes an answer to "why?" using attachment theory and relational goal pursuit theory. As competence experts, the authors explore aspects of relationship management as a way to cope. Particularly useful to teaching is the information on motives, process, and the typology of stalking and ORI tactics.

22 Daly, J. A., McCroskey, J. C., Ayres, J., Hopf, T., & Ayres, D. M. (Eds.). (1997). *Avoiding communication: Shyness, reticence, and communication apprehension* (2nd ed.). Beverly Hills, CA: Sage.
BF575.B3 A96 1997 Communication
This book offers complete coverage of shyness and reticence in interpersonal communication. It defines terms and outlines research, measurement, treatment, and theoretical explanations of communication avoidance. Read selectively from the seventeen chapters in this anthology as you may need to train yourself about how to appropriately teach these topics in an interpersonal communication course.

23 Delia, J. G., O'Keefe, B. J., & O'Keefe, D. J. (1982). The constructivist approach to communication. In F. E. X. Dance (Ed.), *Human communication theory: Comparative essays* (pp. 147–191). New York, NY: Harper & Row.
BF637.C45H85 Communication
This chapter is the best general summary of Delia's constructivist approach and includes philosophical foundations, theory and research foci, methodology, research practices, and extensive references. Constructivism is outlined as an interpretive theory where communication is based on "schemes" that help people create social reality through interaction. Central to this approach is an understanding of how one's interpersonal construct system

functions to guide interpretations, select communication strategies, and generally engage social interaction with others.

24 Dindia, K., & Canary, D. (Eds.). (2006). *Sex differences and similarities in communication* (2nd ed.). Mahwah, NJ: Erlbaum.
P96.S48.S49 2006 Communication, Social Psychology
This anthology has done much to neutralize the common assumption that women and men are different and, therefore, cannot communicate effectively with each other. The second edition updates and adds new knowledge in four parts: framing chapters, theories, exploration of communication process, and a section devoted to romance. Because the research presented is based in social interaction, instructors of interpersonal communication can gain a balanced view on a topic that is often approached by students as "men versus women."

25 Dindia, K., & Duck, S. (Eds.). (2000). *Communication and personal relationships.* Chichester, U.K.: Wiley.
HM1116.C65 2000 Communication
This book focuses on current topics that are part of teaching interpersonal communication. In nine chapters, the best names in interpersonal research (e.g., Bochner, Metts, Spitzberg, Baxter) contribute research-based essays on topics such as stalking, disclosure, facework, stories, and cross-sex friendship. Many of the authors approach their topics by asking what they mean and where the research stands.

26 Donohue, W. A. (2006). Managing interpersonal conflict: The mediation promise. In J. G. Oetzel & S. Ting-Toomey (Eds.), *The Sage handbook of conflict communication: Integrating theory, research, and practice* (pp. 211–233). Thousand Oaks, CA: Sage Publications.
HM1126.S24 2006 Communication
This article discusses the explosion of mediation practices across a wide variety of interpersonal and organizational contexts. Donohue focuses on the interpersonal nature of human conflicts and demonstrates that mediation is a useful tool to manage and resolve conflicts. He highlights different mediation techniques and styles and discusses emerging theories that account for the effectiveness of mediation in conflict resolution and conflict management.

27 Fine, M. A., & Harvey, J. H. (Eds.). (2006). *Handbook of divorce and relationship dissolution.* Mahwah, NJ: Erlbaum.
HQ814.H27 2006 Social Psychology, Interdisciplinary
This timely, comprehensive anthology is an excellent resource for two reasons: first, there is not enough coverage of divorce in our teaching materials and second, students from divorced families seek to understand the impact of divorce on parent-child relationships. There are eight parts to this seven-hundred-page tome, but interpersonal communication instructors will benefit most from the sections on causes, consequences, coping, and variations in divorce (e.g., African American divorce).

28 Fitzpatrick, M. (1988). *Between husbands and wives: Communication in marriage.*
    Thousand Oaks, CA: Sage.
    HQ728.F46 1988 Communication
    This well-known empirical study of marriage resulted in the marital types
    Fitzpatrick calls traditional, independents, and separates. The book out-
    lines the research agenda and the three types. The heart of the book ana-
    lyzes how the three marital types predict different outcomes regarding who
    wields power or has control in the marriage, how conflict is managed, how
    partners gain compliance from each other, and the communication of emo-
    tion. Fitzpatrick provides a realistic look at marital structure and commu-
    nication processes.

29 Galvin, K. M., Bylund, Carma L., & Brommel, B. J. (2004). *Family communica-
    tion: Cohesion and change* (6th ed.). Boston, MA: Pearson/Allyn and Bacon.
    HQ734.G19 2004 Communication
    The topic of family is prevalent in student discussion, and this well-known
    text provides depth of understanding of interpersonal process within a fam-
    ily context. Thirteen chapters cover a range of topics: theories, communica-
    tion patterns, roles, conflict, power, and intimacy. Symbolic interaction and
    systems theories provide the basic framing for a descriptive discussion of
    the issues.

30 Gibb, J. (1961). Defensive communication. *Journal of Communication, 11,*
    141–148.
    P87.J6 Communication
    This classic article is the starting point on reducing defensiveness in rela-
    tionships. Although set up as descriptions of communication climates in
    group settings, the characteristics of defensiveness versus supportiveness
    are frequently prescribed as communication strategies in dyads. Gibb dis-
    cusses the following pairs of communication and their effects on interac-
    tion: evaluation and description, control and problem orientation, strategy
    and spontaneity, neutrality and empathy, superiority and equality, certainty
    and provisionalism.

31 Goffman, E. (1959). *The presentation of self in everyday life.* New York, NY:
    Anchor Books.
    HM291.G6 1959 Sociology
    Goffman's most famous book explores the interpersonal implications for
    impression management in social life. Using a dramatist's perspective — life
    is theatre — he demonstrates how people take on roles within work contexts
    to reach goals. The assumption that people have goals and, most often, in-
    teract interpersonally leads to managing an impression through role behav-
    ior. The ethical and moral dimensions of communication are an integral
    part of the study. After forty-five-plus years, this book still makes a strong
    practical impact.

32 Goffman, E. (1967). *Interaction ritual: Essays in face-to-face behavior.* Chicago,
    IL: Aldine.

HM291.G59 Sociology
This ethnography of interaction is based on the premise that face-to-face behavior is ritualized communication that maintains the larger social order. The first essay, "On Face-Work," is the best known and sets the stage for theorizing the concept of facework (see Cupach and Metts in this bibliography). Interpersonal communication teachers will also learn about other concepts by reading the entire book. Particularly relevant are chapters on deference and demeanor, embarrassment, and alienation.

33 Greene, J. O., & Burleson, B. R. (Eds.). (2003). *Handbook of communication and social interaction skills.* Mahwah, NJ: Erlbaum.
HM1111.H36 2003 Communication
This handbook, ideal for a competence- or skills-based course, includes literature reviews with extensive reference lists. Among the interaction skills reviewed, many are typical in interpersonal communication teaching: arguing, emotional support, friendship interaction, parenting, negotiating, and impression management. Although this is a research tool, the benefits for teaching include updated knowledge and a deeper understanding of what *competence* means.

34 Hall, E. T. (1959). *The silent language.* New York, NY: Anchor Books/ Doubleday.
HM258.H245 1990 Anthropology
It is difficult to teach (or read) about nonverbal communication in relationships without reference to Hall's influential book. Many basic concepts about cross-cultural communication, including perceptions of time and space, are part of what Hall calls "the cultural unconscious." These factors influence perceptions and subsequent behavior when people from different cultures attempt to communicate. Much like his contemporary, Erving Goffman, Hall uses examples from his fieldwork to illustrate principles of nonverbal communication.

35 Hecht, M. L. (Ed.). (1998). *Communicating prejudice.* Thousand Oaks, CA: Sage.
HM276.C625 1998 Communication
Part II of this anthology focuses on spheres of prejudice and how prejudice is embedded in communication codes. Contributors include Molefi Asante, on racist language; Lana Rakow and Laura Wackwitz, on communicating sexism; Thomas Nakayama, on ways of communicating heterosexism; Dreama Moon and Garry Rolison, on classism; and Angie Williams and Howard Giles, on ageism. Each of these five chapters is useful as background knowledge for teaching about "isms" and prejudice.

36 Heider, F. (1958). *The psychology of interpersonal relations.* New York, NY: Wiley.
BF636.H383 Social Psychology
Heider was one of the early relational theorists, and this book is the original source on attribution and balance theories, including the P, O, X logical statements that characterize much of the attribution literature. In this

dense explication of what happens when two people engage one another psychologically in a relationship, Heider starts with the knowledge of naïve psychology in order to logically extend intuitive thought to a more explicit scientific approach to relationships. His claim is that common sense (intuitive or naïve psychology) has much to offer science. He unfolds the idea that as people perceive and react to others in their environment, a kind of ordering process that he calls "attribution" occurs. The theoretical model that results is one that looks at the interaction of perception, action, motivation, sentiments, and norms.

37 Hendrick, C., & Hendrick, S. S. (Eds.). (2000). *Close relationships: A sourcebook.* Thousand Oaks, CA: Sage.
HM1106.C55 2000 Social Psychology, Communication
The best-known theorists are represented in the twenty-six chapters of this anthology, which covers most topics taught in interpersonal communication. Chapters are structured as literature reviews and draw primarily on quantitative studies. A sampling of topics includes: friendship, multiracial dyads, family, gay/lesbian/bisexual dyads, emotion, conflict, gender, attachment, love, aging, social support, jealousy, depression, and aggression.

38 Jourard, S. M. (1971). *The transparent self* (Rev. ed.). New York, NY: Van Nostrand Reinhold. (Original work published 1964)
BF697.J65 1971 Clinical Psychology
Based on the premise that self-disclosure is related to positive health, Jourard's study of transparency is the exemplar of ideas that were swept up in the 1960s humanism movement in interpersonal communication. Historically, this book laid the groundwork for much of our teaching and changed our thinking about the nature and function of self-disclosure. Although it was intended as a tool for use in mental health settings, communication teachers can learn much about relational aspects of self-disclosure that can be applied to healthy dyads. The book also includes Jourard's Self-Disclosure Questionnaire.

39 Kellett, P. M., & Dalton, D. G. (2001). *Managing conflict in a negotiated world: A narrative approach to achieving dialogue and change.* Thousand Oaks, CA: Sage.
HM1126.K45 2001 Communication
Designed as a teaching tool, this book is about analyzing and responding to real-life stories of interpersonal conflict. The first half of the book uses personal narratives as the basis for learning how to dissect conflict and then engage dialogue to negotiate change in personal relationships. The second half of the book devotes chapters to conflicts in community, work, and family. The interpretive perspective framing this book is a significant alternative to most behavioral strategies models used in teaching about conflict.

40 Kirkpatrick, D. C., Duck, S., & Foley, M. K. (Eds.). (2006). *Relating difficulty: The processes of constructing and managing difficult interaction.* Mahwah, NJ: Erlbaum.

BF637.I48.R45 2006 Communication, Sociology, Psychology
Part of Erlbaum's Series on Personal Relationships, this anthology includes twelve chapters that contribute to a more complex notion of what a "difficult" person is and how that impacts relationships. Scholars take on topics such as shyness, in-laws, long distance, money, hook-up experiences, gossip, and chronic illness to explore difficult experiences in relationships. We learn that difficulty is not as simple as dealing with personalities; rather, all the studies point toward a triangulation principle: two people in the dyad are influenced by an outside factor such as a situation or other people. Thus, competent relating requires managing the interaction process rather than attributes of people.

41 Knapp, M. L. (1978). Stages of coming together and coming apart. In *Social intercourse: From greeting to goodbye* (pp. 1–29). Boston, MA: Allyn and Bacon.
HM132.K5 Communication
This is the first version of Knapp's often-used model of interaction stages, which describes growth and decay in interpersonal relationships. In this chapter the reader can see the influence of Altman and Taylor's social penetration theory. This historical essay is the precursor to Knapp's current version in his text with Anita Vangelisti entitled *Interpersonal Communication and Human Relationships.*

42 Knapp, M. L., & Daly, J. A. (Eds.). (2002). *Handbook of interpersonal communication* (3rd ed.). Thousand Oaks, CA: Sage.
BF637.C45 H287 2002 Communication
Like the two previous editions, the *Handbook* is considered a top-notch compilation of interpersonal communication research. Nineteen chapters are divided among five parts: basic issues and approaches, perspectives on inquiry, fundamental units, processes and functions, and contexts. The first chapter, on background and trends, provides historical information and themes to help frame thinking about the field in general. Looking at all three editions of the *Handbook* side by side will also show how the research on interpersonal communication has evolved in the last twenty years.

43 Knapp, M. L., Hart, R. P., & Dennis, H. S. (1974). An exploration of deception as a communication construct. *Human Communication Research, 1,* 15–29.
P91.3H85 Communication
This historical essay sets up some early baseline behaviors for the communication of deception. Empirical testing yielded support for both verbal and nonverbal behaviors used by deceivers in six categories of communication: uncertainty, vagueness, nervousness, reticence, dependence, and negative affect. At least fourteen communication differences were found between deceivers and nondeceivers. After this article, Knapp continued to lead the field in research on deception.

44 Lee, J. A. (1976). *The colors of love.* Englewood Cliffs, NJ: Prentice-Hall/ Psychology Today.
BF575.L8 L33 1976 Sociology

Lee is the originator of the highly popular "lovestyles" theory derived from his study involving extensive interviews of two-hundred-plus men and women about their love experiences. Using themes that emerged from the interviews, Lee developed the five styles of eros, ludus, storge, mania, and agape. He frames and interprets these styles using literature from Western civilization. The book is an in-depth explanation of the five styles of love, both separately and in some form of combination. It includes Lee's lovestyles instrument, allowing the reader to gauge his or her preferred style.

45 Leeds-Hurwitz, W. (Ed.). (1995). *Social approaches to communication.* New York, NY: Guilford.
HM258.S58 1995 Communication
This research anthology is one of the first to synthesize social—also known as interpretive—approaches to theorizing about interpersonal communication. The reader can understand the philosophy, methodology, and controversial politics surrounding interpretation as it came into vogue in our field during the 1990s. An application section includes chapters that can help an instructor make decisions about using case studies, ethnographies, and narratives as instructional strategies to study interpersonal relationships and communication process.

46 Luft, J. (1969). *Of human interaction.* Palo Alto, CA: National Press Books.
HM133.L83 Social Psychology, Personality
Of all his writings, this is Luft's most clear source on the Johari Window, which he first developed in 1955 with Harry Ingham as a tool for self-awareness. This book is organized around the four quadrants of the window: open, blind, hidden, and unknown. Implications for interpersonal learning are played out through such concepts as trust, miscommunication, leadership patterns, and self-disclosure.

47 Martin, J. N., Nakayama, T. K., & Flores, L. A. (Eds.). (2002). *Readings in intercultural communication: Experiences and contexts* (2nd ed.). Boston, MA: McGraw-Hill.
GN345.6 R43 2001 Communication
Intercultural communication is a specific kind of interpersonal communication process that involves much of the diversity that characterizes relationships in today's world. Many perspectives represent a range of cultural experience in these short chapters, but the editors use dialectical theory to broadly frame intercultural communication. This is a rich resource that can expand your approach to teaching about ethics, conflict, language, nonverbal communication, and identity; it also provides classroom activities.

48 Marwell, G., & Schmitt, D. R. (1967). Dimensions of compliance-gaining behavior: An empirical analysis. *Sociometry, 39,* 350–364.
HM1.S8 1 Sociology
This classic study was the first empirical attempt to distinguish clusters of strategies in interpersonal compliance-gaining situations. The authors

found that sixteen strategies clustered around five factors: rewarding activity, punishing activity, expertise, activation of impersonal commitments, and activation of personal commitments. These results correlated positively with French and Raven's power typology. Although much research has been conducted on how partners influence each other to comply and, concomitantly, to resist influence to comply, the sixteen original strategies are still in use today.

49 Miller, G. R., & Steinberg, M. (1975). *Between people: A new analysis of interpersonal communication*. Chicago, IL: Science Research Associates.
HM132.M52 Communication
Between People made a strong impact on the understanding and teaching of interpersonal communication when it was first published, and it is still referenced today. Because it was designed as a textbook, the content of the ten chapters is both descriptive and prescriptive. In framing relationships, the authors define interpersonal relationships as a mutual dyadic system in which thinking (cognitive) partners control their choices through communication skills to achieve outcomes in a given social environment. Historically, the book is an important look at many early concepts (trust, empathy, disclosure, conflict, transaction) that set the stage for how we teach undergraduates about relationships and communication.

50 Mortensen, C. D., with Ayres, C. M. (1997). *Miscommunication*. Thousand Oaks, CA: Sage.
P90.M66 1997 Communication
The term *miscommunication* has been popularized by sociolinguist Deborah Tannen, and students commonly think of it as a cross-sex pattern. Mortensen's book is an in-depth and complex communication model of what happens when people miscommunicate. His analysis is based on personal accounts from eighty participants, and examples from the accounts are used throughout the book. What Mortensen accomplishes is an extended definition of miscommunication, including conditions that precipitate and aggravate negativity.

51 Neuliep, J. W. (2012). *Intercultural communication: A contextual approach* (5th ed.). Los Angeles, CA: Sage.
Communication
This text offers a comprehensive view of culture in interpersonal relationships through examining the microcultural, environmental, socio-relational and perceptual contexts of cultural interactions. The text offers useful information on both the nonverbal and verbal aspects of culture with emphasis on body language, eye contact, message exchange, stages of intercultural relationships, intercultural conflict, stages of culture shock, and so forth. It is a great resource for expanding the discussion of intercultural relationships in any interpersonal communication course.

52 Nofsinger, R. E. (1991). *Everyday conversation*. Newbury Park, CA: Sage.
BJ2121.N64 1991 Communication

Nofsinger presents a highly technical but very readable explication of conversation from a discourse analysis perspective. Through its use of real conversation, the book dispels the assumption that "everyone can communicate." In order to show how conversation works, chapters are organized to build off each other. An introduction on pragmatics leads to conversational action (speech acts) followed by chapters on action sequences, turn organization, and alignment. The last chapter deals with extended structures such as argument, storytelling, and relationships themselves.

53 O'Hair, D., Friedrich, G. W., Wiemann, J. M., & Wiemann, M. O. (1997). *Competent communication* (2nd ed.). New York, NY: St. Martin's.
P90.C63467 1997 Communication
In this hybrid textbook, Parts One and Two comprise six chapters on basic communication processes and three chapters on interpersonal communication. Of note is the competence perspective that extends John Wiemann's work on the definition and components of relational competence. Rather than locating competence only in the individual communicators, Wiemann conceives of the dyad itself as competent. This was a major leap forward in conceptualizing the totality of interpersonal communication.

54 Orbe, M. P. (1998). *Constructing co-cultural theory: An explication of culture, power, and communication.* Thousand Oaks, CA: Sage.
HM258.O63 1998 Communication
Co-cultural theory extends muted group and standpoint theories by looking at communication interaction initiated by co-cultural group members in the direction of dominant group members. Orbe documents twenty-six co-cultural strategies in Chapter 4 and then interprets co-cultural communication in Chapter 5 in terms of assimilation, accommodation, and separation. This useful typology of communication strategies helps students see how the choice of strategy changes the power dynamics in personal relationships involving dominant and socially marginalized partners.

55 Petronio, S. (Ed.). (2000). *Balancing the secrets of private disclosures.* Mahwah, NJ: Erlbaum.
BF697.5 .S427 B35 2000 Communication
This anthology of twenty chapters captures current knowledge on secrets and disclosures by framing the topic through the dialectical idea of private needs versus public exposure. The first three chapters provide an introduction and review of the literature by Lawrence Rosenfeld, Kathryn Dindia, and Sandra Petronio. More specialized chapters follow, including explorations of disclosure in health care contexts, in close relationships, and across cultures.

56 Philipsen, G. (1975). Speaking "like a man" in Teamsterville: Culture patterns of role enactment in an urban neighborhood. *Quarterly Journal of Speech, 61,* 13–22.
PN4071.Q3 Communication

One of the earliest and most influential ethnographic studies of relationships, communication, and gender, Philipsen's study is still current. By discovering cultural rules of community, we can know how talk manifests social identity that is characterized by relationship status, SES, geographical boundaries, gender, and cultural values. Public and private places such as taverns, community centers, and the streets are bound by rules as well, and require competent knowledge by community members in order for relationships to function smoothly. Readers learn that competence is not just a matter of learning skills; rather, skills are implemented in social interaction to be effective.

57 Planalp, S., & Honeycutt, J. M. (1985). Events that increase uncertainty in personal relationships. *Human Communication Research, 11*, 593–604.
P91.3H85 Communication
This study shows how uncertainty arises beyond initial interaction and what partners do to reduce uncertainty in friendship, marriage, and romance. Six types of events produced uncertainty in participants' experience: competing relationships, loss of closeness, sexual behavior, deception, change in personality, and betraying confidence. Results showed the emotional impact to be high and that communication strategies used included talking over and around the issue, arguing, and avoiding both the issue and the partner. This study shows that coping with uncertainty is as important as reducing uncertainty.

58 Rawlins, W. K. (1992). *Friendship matters: Communication, dialectics, and the life course.* Hawthorne, NY: Aldine de Gruyter.
HM132.5 R38 1992 Communication
Not only is this one of the earliest and best studies of friendship in the field of communication, but Rawlins also grounds his work in relational dialectics theory. Using one hundred interviews as the basis of his data collection, Rawlins examines the tensions of friendships throughout life, including a look at children, adolescents, young adults, and older adults. Four dialectical tensions emerge to characterize communication processes in friendship: independent-dependent, affection-instrumentality, judgment-acceptance, and expressiveness-protectiveness.

59 Rogers, C. R. (1995). *On becoming a person: A therapist's view of psychotherapy* (P. D. Kramer, intro.). Boston, MA: Houghton Mifflin. (Original work published 1961)
RC480.5 R62 1995 Clinical Psychology
Rogers's famous humanistic look at the client-therapist relationship is actually a collection of thirty years' worth of his writing. Lessons are given on self-awareness, empathy, relational understanding, and unconditional positive regard for others as conditions of self-actualization, or becoming a person. Of the seven parts of the book, Parts I, II, III, IV, and VI explicate Rogers's philosophy and method of approaching interpersonal relationships.

60 Roloff, M. E. (1981). *Interpersonal communication: The social exchange approach.*
    Beverly Hills, CA: Sage.
    HM132.R653 Communication
    This book has a single focus on five theories under the umbrella of social
    exchange. The reader is able to clarify the contributions of the Operant
    Psychology Approach, the Economic Exchange Model, the Theory of In-
    terdependence, Resource Theory, and Equity Theory as they relate to the
    theoretical concept that humans engage in social exchange as a fundamen-
    tal process of relating. Roloff compares the assumptions of each theory,
    looks at how each theory views various interpersonal processes (relational
    development, self-disclosure, and conflict), and gauges strengths and weak-
    nesses of each.

61 Roloff, M. E., & Berger, C. R. (Eds.). (1982). *Social cognition and communication.*
    Beverly Hills, CA: Sage.
    HM132.S566 1982 Communication
    In nine chapters, this anthology defines social cognition, explicates the
    relationship between social cognition and communication, and then ap-
    plies the whole process to the following areas: impression formation and
    message production, attribution, relational trajectories in friendship and
    love, speech accommodation, legal trials, organizations, and mass commu-
    nication. The first chapter by Roloff and Berger is known as one of the best
    statements in the field on what social cognition is ("organized thoughts
    people have about human interaction") and how it works.

62 Rosenfeld, L. B. (1979). Self-disclosure avoidance: Why I am afraid to tell
    you who I am. *Communication Monographs, 46,* 63–74.
    PN4077.S6 Communication
    This study is a favorite in self-disclosure literature and among students.
    Instead of the usual "what" and "how much" approach, Rosenfeld empir-
    ically investigates why men and women avoid disclosing. Results from
    self-disclosure and avoidance measures showed similarity on avoiding dis-
    closure so as not to project an undesired image, but there were also sex dif-
    ferences. Males primarily avoid disclosure so as not to lose control of the
    dyad, while females avoid disclosure so that information would not be used
    against them.

63 Ruesch, J., & Bateson, G. (1951). *Communication: The social matrix of psychiatry.*
    New York, NY: Norton.
    RC602.R9 Psychiatry, Anthropology
    This historic book is one of the first systematic (scientific) theories of inter-
    personal communication and the original source for the term *metacommuni-
    cation.* Using a systems perspective, Ruesch (a psychiatrist) and Bateson (an
    anthropologist) locate interpersonal communication in dyads that func-
    tion within a larger American social matrix. Communication is seen as an
    integrated system of information, cybernetics, cultural values, human inter-
    action, and wholeness. The "levels of communication" model is also one of

the first contextual conceptualizations of communication as intrapersonal, interpersonal, group, and cultural.

64 Sass, C. P. (1994). On interpersonal competence. In K. Carter & M. Presnell (Eds.), *Interpretive approaches to interpersonal communication* (pp. 137–157). Albany, NY: SUNY Press.
BF637.N66I68 1994 Communication
Using a symbolic interaction framework, Sass develops an interpretive model of interpersonal competence. She theoretically teases out "the social interaction of the individuals." Three assumptions (reflexivity, context, unification) ground her definition of *competence*. Competence is viewed as relational, mutually satisfactory, authentic, and having shared perception between partners. This interpretive model is an alternative to the more common behavioral approach to competence.

65 Satir, V. (1972). *Peoplemaking*. Palo Alto, CA: Science and Behavior Books.
HQ734.S266 Clinical Psychology
Satir is a family therapist whose work has been adopted by interpersonal communication teachers and trainers. In concentrating on healthy family process, she uses four key concepts: self-worth, communication, systems, and rules. Communicating in family relationships is overt or implied on virtually every page of the book, but Chapters 4, 5, and 6 concentrate on communication processes, including the famous patterns of placate, blame, compute, and distract.

66 Schutz, W. C. (1966). *The interpersonal underworld*. Palo Alto, CA: Science and Behavior Books. (Originally published in 1958 as *FIRO: A three-dimensional theory of interpersonal behavior*)
HM132.S38 1966 Psychiatry
This highly empirical book presents Schutz's well-known theory of Fundamental Interpersonal Relations Orientation (FIRO). His simple contention that "people need people" is manifested in the three basic needs of inclusion, control, and affection (in that order). Further, he proposes that we both give ("expressed behavior") and receive ("wanted behavior") these basic needs. Compatibility is linked to these needs as a predictor of successful relationships. The FIRO-B questionnaire is included as Chapter 4.

67 Shotter, J. (1993). *Conversational realities: Constructing life through language*. Thousand Oaks, CA: Sage.
P95.45.S56 1993 Communication, Psychology
A well-known social constructionist, Shotter offers a book that centers on the way language helps us construct interpersonal relationships. Shotter claims that communication interaction creates social life (reality) by revealing how we relate to each other and then make sense of our lives through that talk. His evidence for the claim is conversation analysis and a complicated synthesis of literature from psychology, European philosophy, rhetoric, and linguistics. He builds a framework to explain the process of "living dialogue" between people. The value of this book for interpersonal

communication instructors is in being able to see how social construction works as perspective to teach concepts such as dialogue, conversation, and relationships.

68 Simpson, J. A., & Harris, B. A. (1994). Interpersonal attraction. In A. L. Weber & J. H. Harvey (Eds.), *Perspectives on close relationships* (pp. 45-66). Boston, MA: Allyn and Bacon.
BF511.P46 1994 Social Psychology
This chapter does an excellent job of summarizing the basic concepts of Ellen Berscheid's and Harold Kelley's original works on attraction. Using Kelley's model, the content of this chapter is divided into the P, E, O, and P X O variables that represent the four categories of variables that influence attraction. P variables are attributes a person brings to the situation; E variables are environmental influences; O variables are attributes of the other person; and P X O variables are the intersecting attributes of the two people. Familiar concepts within these categories include expectancies, proximity, attractiveness, and similarity.

69 Spitzberg, B. H., & Cupach, W. R. (1984). *Interpersonal communication competence*. Beverly Hills, CA: Sage.
BF637.C45 S67 1984 Communication
A compact overview of concepts and theories in interpersonal communication, this primer has served the field heuristically in teaching and research. A conceptual model based on five components in interaction is offered to organize the literature on competence: motivation, knowledge, skills, context, and outcomes. A short discussion in the last chapter considers pedagogical implications.

70 Stafford, L., & Canary, D. J. (1991). Maintenance strategies and romantic relationship type, gender and relational characteristics. *Journal of Social and Personal Relationships, 8*, 217-242.
Communication
This classic study reveals the five maintenance strategies frequently cited in interpersonal communication textbooks including positivity, assurances, openness, sharing tasks, and social networks. The findings also suggest important relationship implications of relational maintenance such as control mutuality, commitment, satisfaction, and liking.

71 Sternberg, R, J. (1988). *The triangle of love: Intimacy, passion, commitment*. New York, NY: Basic Books.
BF575.L8 S78 1988 Social Psychology
Sternberg presents a social psychological theory of love based on the three factors of intimacy, passion, and commitment. Eight chapters include valuable discussions of attraction, liking versus loving, and the course of a relationship. Chapter 2, "The Ingredients of Love," offers a detailed explication of the theory. The Sternberg Triangular Love Scale, presented in Chapter 3, could be a basis for class data collection and analysis.

72 Suler, J. (2004). The online disinhibition effect. *CyberPsychology & Behavior*, 7(3), 321–326.
Psychology
Suler's work helps us understand computer-mediated communication in interpersonal interactions. Suler described the online disinhibition effect as the phenomenon "when people say and do things in cyberspace that they wouldn't ordinarily say and do in the face-to-face world." This can result in positive behaviors (benign disinhibition) or negative behaviors (toxic disinhibition). Six factors attribute to the disinhibition effect: dissociative anonymity, invisibility, asynchronicity, solipsistic introjection, dissociative imagination, and minimization of status and authority.

73 Thibaut, J. W., & Kelley, H. H. (1986/2004). *The social psychology of groups*. New Brunswick, NJ: Transaction. (Original work published 1959)
HM131.T46 1986 Social Psychology
This is the original source of what most interpersonal texts call "social exchange theory." Thibaut and Kelley, however, call their explanation "interdependence theory" and maintain the idea that dyads are the basis of all social interaction where partners create patterns of interdependence in controlling outcomes. Chapters 1 through 10 lay out the theory, including explication of cost, rewards, CL, CLalt, power, and the outcome matrix. Their 1978 book, *Interpersonal Relations*, takes the theory out of a group context and more explicitly develops the dyadic implications.

74 Van Dijk, T. A. (1987). *Communicating racism: Ethnic prejudice in thought and talk*. Newbury Park, CA: Sage.
HM291.D496 1987 Communication
Based on interview data from Amsterdam and San Diego, this study examines how whites reproduce racism in everyday talk. Using discourse analysis, Van Dijk theorizes how prejudiced discourse is structured, how we cognitively organize prejudice, and, most important, how racism is communicated in interpersonal interaction. Although deeply detailed, this book provides a strong foundation for understanding racism as a social phenomenon manifested in communication among people.

75 Vangelisti, A. L. (Ed.). (2004). *Handbook of family communication*. Mahwah, NJ: Erlbaum.
HQ519.H36 2003 Communication
This textbook written by several experts includes thirty chapters covering a variety of topics within a specific interpersonal context: family relationships. The book includes six units highlighting the work from a variety of disciplines including: (1) family definitions, theories and methods, (2) communication across the family life course, (3) communication in various family forms, (4) the relational communication of family members, (5) family communication processes, and (6) communication and contemporary family issues. The book concludes with a look at the challenges and decisions families will face in the future.

76 Vangelisti, A. L., Daly, J. A., & Friedrich, G. W. (Eds.). (1999). *Teaching communication: Theory, research, and methods* (2nd ed.). Mahwah, NJ: Erlbaum.
P91.3 T43 1999 Communication, Pedagogy
Written by experts in the field, this thirty-eight-chapter general resource offers various pieces of advice ranging from professionalism to course creation to instructional strategies to evaluation techniques. This advice is particularly valuable because it is contextualized within the communication field. The chapter on teaching interpersonal communication offers a good starting point for thinking about course design.

77 Walster, E., Walster, G. W., & Berscheid, E. (1978). *Equity: Theory and research.* Boston: Allyn and Bacon.
HM251.W2658 Social Psychology
This is the definitive source on equity theory. Framed as a general theory, it examines notions of fairness in human relationships. Chapter 2 explicates the four basic propositions of equity theory: we maximize outcomes (1) as individuals and (2) in groups; (3) inequity equals distress; and (4) people in distress try to restore equity. Separate chapters apply the theory to four types of relationships: exploiter/victim, philanthropist/recipient, business, and intimate. The book concludes with its own theoretical critique. Despite the common tendency to treat equity theory as an extension or alternative to social exchange theory, it is conceptually distinct.

78 Walther, J. B. (1992). Interpersonal effects in computer-mediated interaction: A relational perspective. *Communication Research, 19,* 52–90.
Communication
Early computer-mediated communication (CMC) research initially indicated that online communication could not transmit the same amount of information that was learned in face-to-face interpersonal communication due to the absence of nonverbal cues. As a result, people thought that relationships could not be initiated or maintained via online communication. In this foundational essay on CMC, Walther criticizes this early research. He explains that CMC can, in fact, accomplish the same amount of information as face-to-face communication can—but CMC takes more time to achieve the same level of transmitted information. Walther explored this phenomenon further, labeling his theory Social Information Processing (SIP).

79 Walther, J. B. (1996). Computer-mediated communication: Impersonal, interpersonal, and hyperpersonal interaction. *Communication Research, 23*(1), 3–44.
Communication
Walther argues that CMC can be impersonal, interpersonal, and hyperpersonal. Walther proposed the hyperpersonal model to explain the ability for someone to develop a more intimate (hyperpersonal) relationship with someone via CMC versus face-to-face communication. He attributes this effect to four elements of CMC: (1) the message receiver inflating

perceptions formed about his or her partner; (2) the message sender optimizing his or her self-presentation; (3) the asynchronous channel allowing for editability and convenience; and (4) an intensified feedback loop.

80 Watzlawick, P., Bavelas, J. B., & Jackson, D. D. (1967). *Pragmatics of human communication*. New York, NY: Norton.
BF637.C45 W3 Clinical Psychology
No other book has had more influence on the teaching of interpersonal communication than *Pragmatics*, particularly the five axioms in Chapter 2. The book broke new ground as the authors used their powers of behavioral observation to construct a "calculus," or model of interpersonal relationships, from a systems perspective. Although dense at times, the book contains now-familiar concepts: paradox or double bind, metacommunication, complementarity, symmetrical structure, and message punctuation. The book also includes an application to *Who's Afraid of Virginia Woolf?*

81 West, S. G., & Wicklund, R. A. (1980). *A primer of social psychological theories*. Monterey, CA: Brooks/Cole.
HM251.W573 Social Psychology
Part Three in this concept-oriented text has three chapters on attribution theory: Self-Perception Theory, the Theory of Correspondent Inferences, and Kelley's Attribution Theory. In about fifty pages, the book provides a solid discussion of the process of attribution, or how we assign causation to behavior — one of the top social cognition concepts taught in interpersonal communication courses.

82 Wilmot, W. W., & Hocker, J. L. (2006). *Interpersonal conflict* (7th ed.). New York, NY: McGraw-Hill.
HM1121.H62 2006 Communication, Clinical Psychology
Conflict is one of the most popular areas of interest to students, and this text provides in-depth coverage on the topic. In addition to the expected chapters on definition, power, styles, and negotiation, there is a chapter on forgiveness and reconciliation. The book is informative and practical from a skills-based perspective, and includes many applications for classroom use.

83 Wood, J. T. (Ed.). (1996). *Gendered relationships*. Mountain View, CA: Mayfield Publishing.
HQ1075.G467 1995 Communication, Psychology
Wood's goal to "focus specifically on [the] reciprocal influence between gender and relationships" is met in this fifteen-chapter anthology divided into four parts: foundations, personal relationships, romance, and professional relationships. Particularly useful are the chapters on friendship, lesbian/gay romance, violence, sexual harassment, and workplace issues. This book can be used as both a primary text and a source of supplemental reading.

84 Wood, J. T. (2000). Relational culture: The nucleus of intimacy. In *Relational communication: Continuity and change in personal relationships* (2nd ed., pp. 76–100). Belmont, CA: Wadsworth.

BF637.C45 W66 1999 Communication
This chapter is a full realization of the ideas on relational culture that Wood first drafted in a 1982 *Communication Quarterly* essay. The chapter looks at relational dialectics; organizing structures; rules; and symbolic practices such as rituals, routines, placemaking, and scripts as the components of relational culture. Wood contends that each of these components of relational culture is enacted through communication. She claims that such communication processes, structures, and practices reveal the uniqueness of every relationship we participate in. This chapter provides a practical set of conceptual tools for students to use when analyzing a personal relationship.

85 Wood, J. T., & Duck, S. (Eds.). (1995). *Under-studied relationships: Off the beaten track*. Thousand Oaks, CA: Sage.
HM132.U54 1993 v.6 Communication, Interdisciplinary
Volume Six in the Sage Understanding Relationship Processes Series examines notions of dyadic competence in relationships that had received little research attention at the time. The groundwork here opens the reader to what was known about long-distance communication, cyber relationships, gay-lesbian dyads, long-term marriages, and intracultural minority interaction. Model-building and theoretical framing are common approaches in the eight chapters that constitute the book.

References

Adler, R., Proctor, R. F., & Towne, N. (2005). *Looking out/looking in* (11th ed.). Belmont, CA: Wadsworth.

Albom, M. (1997). *Tuesdays with Morrie*. New York, NY: Doubleday.

Altman, I., & Taylor, D. A. (1983). *Social penetration: The development of interpersonal relationships*. New York, NY: Irvington. (Original work published 1973)

Anderson, L. W., & Krathwohl, D. R. (Eds.). (2001). *A taxonomy for learning, teaching, and assessing: A revision of Bloom's Taxonomy of Educational Objectives*. New York, NY: Longman.

Angelo, T. A., & Cross, K. P. (1993). *Classroom assessment techniques: A handbook for college teachers*. San Francisco, CA: Jossey-Bass.

Applegate, J. L., & Morreale, S. P. (1999). Service-learning in communication: A natural partnership [Preface]. In D. Droge & B. O. Murphy (Eds.), *Voices of a strong democracy: Concepts and models for service-learning in communication studies* (pp. ix–xiv). Washington, DC: American Association for Higher Education.

Artz, L. (2001). Critical ethnography for communication studies: Dialogue and social justice in service-learning. *Southern Communication Journal, 66*, 239–250.

Bain, K. (2004). *What the best college teachers do*. Cambridge, MA: Harvard University Press.

Banta, T. W. (2002). *Building a scholarship of assessment*. San Francisco, CA: Jossey-Bass.

Barnes, S. B. (2003). *Computer-mediated communication: Human-to-human communication across the Internet*. Boston, MA: Allyn & Bacon.

Bateson, M. C. (1989). *Composing a life*. New York, NY: Grove Press.

Baxter, L. A. (1988). A dialectical perspective on communication strategies in relationship development. In S. W. Duck, D. F. Hay, S. E. Hobfoll, W. Iches, & B. Montgomery (Eds.), *Handbook of personal relationships* (pp. 257–273). Chichester, U.K.: Wiley.

Baxter, L. A. (1990). Dialectical contradictions in relationship development. *Journal of Social and Personal Relationships, 7*, 69–88.

Baxter, L. A., & Montgomery, B. M. (1996). *Relating: Dialogues and dialectics*. New York, NY: Guilford.

Baxter, L. A., & Montgomery, B. M. (2000). Rethinking communication in personal relationships from a dialectical perspective. In K. Dindia & S. Duck (Eds.), *Communication and personal relationships* (pp. 31–53). Chichester, U.K.: Wiley.

Bean, J. C. (1996). *Engaging ideas: The professor's guide to integrating writing, critical thinking, and active learning in the classroom*. San Francisco, CA: Jossey-Bass.

Beebe, S., Beebe, S., & Redmond, M. (2005). *Interpersonal communication: Relating to others* (4th ed.). Boston, MA: Allyn & Bacon.

Bender, T. (2003). *Discussion-based online teaching to enhance student learning: Theory, practice and assessment*. Sterling, VA: Stylus Publishing.

Berger, P. L., & Luckmann, T. (1966). *The social construction of reality: A treatise in the sociology of knowledge*. New York, NY: Anchor Books.

Bloom, B. S. (Ed.), Engelhart, M. D., Furst, E. J., Hill, W. H., & Krathwohl, D. R. (1956). *Taxonomy of educational objectives: The classification of educational goals, by a committee of college and university examiners.* New York, NY: Longmans, Green.

Bochner, A. P. (1994). Perspectives on inquiry II: Theories and stories. In M. L. Knapp & G. R. Miller (Eds.), *Handbook of interpersonal communication* (2nd ed., pp. 21–41). Thousand Oaks, CA: Sage.

Bohm, D. (2004). *On dialogue.* New York, NY: Routledge.

Buber, M. (1970). *I and thou* (W. Kaufmann, Trans.). New York, NY: Scribner's. (Original work published 1937)

Burke, J. (2005). *A journey of change.* Unpublished manuscript, University of North Carolina at Greensboro.

Buscaglia, L. (1982). *Living, loving, and learning.* New York, NY: Holt, Rinehart, & Winston.

Campbell, D. M. (Ed.). (2004). *How to develop a professional portfolio: A manual for teachers* (3rd ed.). Boston, MA: Allyn and Bacon.

Canary, D. J., Cody, M. J., & Manusov, V. L. (2003). Four important cognitive processes. In K. M. Galvin & P. J. Cooper (Eds.), *Making connections: Readings in relational communication* (pp. 42–51). Los Angeles, CA: Roxbury.

Cannon, L. W. (1989, May). *Meeting diversity in the college classroom.* Workshop presented at the Memphis State University Conference on Gender Balancing the Curriculum.

Carter, K., & Presnell, M. (1994). *Interpretive approaches to interpersonal communication.* Albany, NY: SUNY Press.

Cayanus, J. L. (2004). Using teacher self-disclosure as an instructional tool. *Communication Teacher, 18,* 6–9.

Christ, W. G. (Ed.). (1994). *Assessing communication education: A handbook for media, speech and theatre educators.* Mahwah, NJ: Erlbaum.

Christophel, D. (1990). The relationship among teacher immediacy behaviors, student motivation, and learning. *Communication Education, 39,* 323–340.

Civikly-Powell, J. (1999). Creating a new course. In A. L. Vangelisti, J. A. Daly, & G. W. Friedrich (Eds.), *Teaching communication: Theory, research, and methods* (2nd ed., pp. 61–72). Mahwah, NJ: Erlbaum.

Comstock, J., Rowell, E., & Bowers, J. W. (1995). Food for thought: Teacher nonverbal immediacy, student learning and curvilinearity. *Communication Education, 44,* 251–266.

Confucius. (1979). *The analects.* (D. C. Lau, Trans.). London: Penguin.

Cooper, P. J., & Simonds, C. J. (2003). *Communication for the classroom teacher* (7th ed.). Boston, MA: Allyn and Bacon.

Craig, R. T. (1999). Communication theory as a field. *Communication Theory, 9,* 119–161.

Crowe, J. A., & Karayan, S. (1997, April). Student perceptions of electronic discussion groups. *Technological Horizons in Education Journal, 24*(9), 69–71. Retrieved from http://thejournal.com/articles/1997/04/01/student-perceptions-of-electronic -discussion-groups.aspx.

Curzon, L. B. (2004). *Teaching in further education: An outline of principles and practice* (6th ed.). London: Continuum.

Cushman, D. P., & Kovacic, B. (Eds.). (1995). *Watershed research traditions in human communication theory.* Albany, NY: SUNY Press.

DeVito, J. A. (2004). Interpersonal relationships: Growth and deterioration. In *The interpersonal communication book* (10th ed., pp. 252–279). Boston, MA: Pearson/Allyn & Bacon.

DeVito, J. A. (2004). *The interpersonal communication book* (10th ed.). Boston, MA: Pearson Education.

DeVito, J. A. (2006). *The interpersonal communication book* (11th ed.). Boston, MA: Pearson Education.

Droge, D., & Murphy, B. O. (Eds.). (1999). *Voices of a strong democracy: Concepts and models for service-learning in communication studies.* Washington, DC: American Association for Higher Education.

Duck, S. (1982). A topography of relationship disengagement and dissolution. In S. Duck (Ed.), *Personal relationships 4: Dissolving personal relationships* (pp. 1–29). London: Academic Press.

Earnest, William. (2010). *Save our slides: PowerPoint design that works.* Dubuque, IA: Kendall Hunt.

Etzioni, A. (1996). *The new golden rule: Community and morality in a democratic society.* New York, NY: Basic Books.

Farrell, T. B. (1987). Beyond science: Humanities contributions to communication theory. In C. R. Berger & S. H. Chaffee (Eds.), *Handbook of communication science* (pp. 123–139). Newbury Park, CA: Sage.

Feeley, T. H. (2002). Evidence of halo effects in student evaluations of communication instruction. *Communication Education, 51,* 225–236.

Filene, P. (2005). *The joy of teaching.* Chapel Hill: University of North Carolina Press.

Finkelstein, J. E. (2006). *Learning in real time: Synchronous teaching and learning online.* San Francisco, CA: Jossey-Bass.

Friedrich, G. W., & Cooper, P. (1999). The first day. In A. L. Vangelisti, J. A. Daly, & G. W. Friedrich (Eds.), *Teaching communication: Theory, research, and methods* (2nd ed., pp. 287–296). Mahwah, NJ: Erlbaum.

Frymier, A. B., & Houser, M. L. (2000). The teacher-student relationship as an interpersonal relationship. *Communication Education, 49,* 207–219.

Fulghum, R. (1989). *All I really need to know I learned in kindergarten: Uncommon thoughts on common things.* New York, NY: Villard Books.

Gerbner, G. (1990). Epilogue: Advancing on the path of righteousness (maybe). In N. Signorielli & M. Morgan (Eds.), *Cultivation analysis: New directions in media effects research* (pp. 249–262). Newbury Park, CA: Sage.

Gibb, J. (1961). Defensive communication. *Journal of Communication, 11,* 141–148.

Glater, J. D. (2006, February 21). To: Professor@university.edu subject: Why it's all about me. *New York Times.* Retrieved from http://www.nytimes.com.

Goffman, E. (1959). *The presentation of self in everyday life.* New York, NY: Anchor Books.

Goldstein, G. S., & Benassi, V. A. (1994). The relation between teacher self-disclosure and student classroom participation. *Teaching of Psychology, 21,* 212–216.

Graham, E. E., & Shue, C. K. (2001). Reflections on the past, directions for the future: A template for the study and instruction of interpersonal communication. *Communication Research Reports, 18.* (Reprinted from *CRR, 17,* pp. 337–348. Volume 18 is the complete version with the same page numbers as Volume 17.)

Gronlund, N. E., & Linn, R. L. (1990). *Measurement and evaluation in teaching* (6th ed.). New York, NY: Macmillan.

Grunert, J. (1997). *The course syllabus: A learning-centered approach.* Bolton, MA: Anker.

Gulley, H. E. (1968). *Discussion, conference, and group process* (2nd ed.). New York, NY: Holt, Rinehart and Winston.

Gunawardena, C. N., & Zittle, F. J. (1997). Social presence as a predictor of satisfaction within a computer-mediated conferencing environment. *American Journal of Distance Education, 11*(3), 8–26.

Hayakawa, S. I., & Hayakawa, A. R. (1992). *Language in thought and action* (5th ed.). Fort Worth, TX: Harcourt Brace.

Hendrix, K. G. (2000). *The teaching assistant's guide to the basic course.* Belmont, CA: Wadsworth.

Higgins, R. (1994). Classroom management and organization. In K. W. Prichard & R. M. Sawyer (Eds.), *Handbook of college teaching: Theory and applications* (pp. 403–414). Westport, CT: Greenwood.

Houser, M. L. (2004). Understanding instructional communication needs of nontraditional students. *Communication Teacher, 18,* 78–81.

Howard, R. (Producer/Director). (2001). *A beautiful mind* [Motion picture]. United States: Universal Studios.

Intrator, S. (Ed.). (2002). *Stories of the courage to teach: Honoring the teacher's heart.* San Francisco, CA: Jossey-Bass.

Jones, E. A. (1994). *Essential skills in writing, speech and listening, and critical thinking for college graduates: Perspectives of faculty, employers, and policymakers.* University Park, PA: National Center for Postsecondary Teaching, Learning, and Assessment.

Jourard, S. M. (1971). *The transparent self* (Rev. ed.). New York, NY: Van Nostrand Reinhold. (Original work published 1964)

Kennedy, G. A. (Ed. & Trans.). (1991). *Aristotle on rhetoric: A theory of civic discourse.* New York, NY: Oxford University Press.

Kibler, R. J., Barker, L. L., & Miles, D. T. (1970). *Behavioral objectives and instruction.* Boston, MA: Allyn & Bacon.

Knapp, M. L., & Daly, J. A. (Eds.). (2002). *Handbook of interpersonal communication* (3rd ed.). Thousand Oaks, CA: Sage.

Knapp, M. L., & Vangelisti, A. L. (1992). Stages of coming together and coming apart. In *Interpersonal communication and human relationships* (2nd ed., pp. 29–63). Boston, MA: Allyn & Bacon.

Knapp, M. L., & Vangelisti, A. L. (2005). Stages of coming together and coming apart. In *Interpersonal communication and human relationships* (5th ed., pp. 31–67). Boston, MA: Allyn & Bacon.

Krathwohl, D. R. (2002). A revision of Bloom's taxonomy: An overview. *Theory into Practice, 41,* 212–218.

Laing, R. D. (1969). *Self and others.* London: Tavistock.

Lawson, Karen. (1999). *Involving your audience: Making it active.* Boston, MA: Allyn & Bacon.

Leeds-Hurwitz, W. (Ed.). (1995). *Social approaches to communication.* New York, NY: Guilford.

Lucas, R. W. (2005). *People strategies for trainers: 176 tips and techniques for dealing with difficult classroom situations.* New York, NY: Amacom.

Luft, J. (1969). *Of human interaction.* Palo Alto, CA: National Press Books.

McCarthy, C. (1998). *Cities of the plain.* New York, NY: Knopf.

McCornack, Steven. (2012). *Reflect & relate: An introduction to interpersonal communication.* New York, NY: Bedford/St. Martin's.

McKeachie, W. J. (1969). *Teaching tips: A guidebook for the beginning college teacher* (6th ed.). Lexington, MA: Heath.

Mead, G. H. (1934). *Mind, self and society.* Chicago, IL: University of Chicago Press.

Mehrabian, A. (1971). *Silent messages.* Belmont, CA: Wadsworth.

Miller, K. (2002). *Communication theories: Perspectives, processes, and contexts.* Boston, MA: McGraw-Hill.

Moore, A., Masterson, J. T., Christophel, D. M., & Shea, K. A. (1996). College teacher immediacy and student ratings of instruction. *Communication Education, 45,* 29–39.

Morreale, S., & Backlund, P. M. (1999). Assessment: Coming of age. *Popular Measurement. Journal of the Institute for Objective Measurement, 2*(1), 22–23.

Natalle, E. J. (2003, September). *Teaching excellence and the Confucian ideal.* College of Arts and Sciences Teaching Excellence Award Lecture, University of North Carolina at Greensboro.

Natalle, E. J., & Bodenheimer, F. R. (2004). *The woman's public speaking handbook.* Belmont, CA: Wadsworth.

Nicholson, J., & Duck, S. (1999). Teaching interpersonal communication. In A. L. Vangelisti, J. A. Daly, & G. W. Friedrich (Eds.), *Teaching communication: Theory, research, and methods* (2nd ed., pp. 85–98). Mahwah, NJ: Erlbaum.

Nussbaum, J. F. (1992). Effective teacher behaviors. *Communication Education, 41,* 167–180.

O'Hair, D., Friedrich, G. W., Wiemann, J. M., & Wiemann, M. O. (1995). *Competent communication.* New York, NY: Bedford/St. Martin's.

Orbe, M. P. (1998). *Constructing co-cultural theory: An explication of culture, power, and communication.* Thousand Oaks, CA: Sage.

Orbe, M. P. (2004). Negotiating multiple identities within multiple frames: An analysis of first-generation college students. *Communication Education, 53,* 131–149.

Orbe, M. P., & Bruess, C. J. (2005). *Contemporary issues in interpersonal communication.* Los Angeles, CA: Roxbury Publishing.

Partridge, J. (n.d.). *Plato's cave and The Matrix.* Retrieved from http://whatisthematrix.warnerbros.com/rl_cmp/new_phil_partridge.html.

Phillips, G. M., & Wood, J. T. (1983). *Communication and human relationships: The study of interpersonal communication.* New York, NY: Macmillan.

Pickering, J. W. (2006, January). Assessment measures: The right tools for the job. Presentation at the University of North Carolina at Greensboro Office of Academic Assessment Workshop, *Assessment, skills, and knowledge: Tools you can use,* Greensboro, NC.

Pilling-Cormick, J., & Garrison, D. R. (2007). Self-directed and self-regulated learning: Conceptual links. *Canadian Journal of University Continuing Education, 33,* 13–33.

Plato. (1985). *The Republic/Plato* (R. W. Sterling & W. C. Scott, Trans.). New York, NY: Norton.

Prichard, K. W., & Sawyer, R. M. (Eds.). (1994). Methods of college instruction. In *Handbook of college teaching: Theory and applications* (pp. 83–84). Westport, CT: Greenwood.

Putnam, R. D. (2000). *Bowling alone: The collapse and revival of American community.* New York, NY: Simon and Schuster.

Quinlan, K. M. (2002). Inside the peer review process: How academics review a colleague's teaching portfolio. *Teaching and Teacher Education, 18,* 1035–1049.

Quintilian. (1965). *On the early education of the citizen-orator* (Rev. J. S. Watson, Trans.). Indianapolis, IN: Bobbs-Merrill.

Rawlins, W. K. (1992). *Friendship matters: Communication, dialectics, and the life course.* Hawthorne, NY: Aldine de Gruyter.

Rawlins, W. K. (2000). Teaching as a mode of friendship. *Communication Theory, 10,* 5–26.

Reid, T. R. (1999). *Confucius lives next door.* New York, NY: Vintage Books.

Richardson, J. C., & Swan, K. Examining social presence in online courses in relation to students' perceived learning and satisfaction. *Journal of Asynchronous Learning, 7(1)*, 68–88.

Rogers, C. R. (1961). *On becoming a person: A therapist's view of psychotherapy.* Boston, MA: Houghton Mifflin.

Roloff, M. E., & Berger, C. R. (Eds.). (1982). *Social cognition and communication.* Beverly Hills, CA: Sage.

Rosen, J. (2003, September 7). How to reignite the culture wars. *New York Times Magazine,* pp. 48ff.

Rubin, R. B. (1995, November). *The undergraduate student canon: Standards and assessment.* Paper presented at the annual meeting of the National Communication Association, San Antonio, TX.

Rubin, R. B. (1999). Evaluating the product. In A. L. Vangelisti, J. A. Daly, & G. W. Friedrich (Eds.), *Teaching communication: Theory, research, and methods* (2nd ed., pp. 425–444). Mahwah, NJ: Erlbaum.

Rubin, R. B., & Morreale, S. P. (1996). Setting expectations for speech communication and listening. In M. Kramer (Series Ed.) & E. A. Jones (Vol. Ed.), *New directions for higher education: Vol. 96. Preparing competent college graduates: Setting new and higher expectations for student learning* (pp. 19–29). San Francisco, CA: Jossey-Bass.

Ruesch, J., & Bateson, G. (1951). *Communication: The social matrix of psychiatry.* New York, NY: Norton.

Salkind, N. J. (2006). *Tests & measurement for people who (think they) hate tests & measurement.* Thousand Oaks, CA: Sage.

Satir, V. (1972). *Peoplemaking.* Palo Alto, CA: Science and Behavior Books.

Schrodt, P. (2003). Students' appraisals of instructors as a function of students' perceptions of instructors' aggressive communication. *Communication Education, 52,* 106–121.

Shepherd, G. J., St. John, J., & Striphas, T. (Eds.). (2006). *Communication as . . . Perspectives on theory.* Thousand Oaks, CA: Sage.

Shuell, T. J., & Farber, S. L. (2001). Students' perceptions of technology use in college courses. *Journal of Educational Computing Research, 24,* 119–138.

Smith, A. L. (1973). *Transracial communication.* Englewood Cliffs, NJ: Prentice-Hall.

Smith, G. G., Ferguson, D. L., & Caris, A. (2001). Teaching college courses online vs face-to-face. *Technological Horizons in Education Journal, 28*(9), 18–24. Retrieved from http://thejournal.com/articles/2001/04/01/teaching-college-courses-online-vs-facetoface.aspx.

Souza, T. (1999). Service-learning and interpersonal communication: Connecting students with the community. In D. Droge & B. O. Murphy (Eds.), *Voices of a strong democracy: Concepts and models for service-learning in communication studies* (pp. 77–86). Washington, DC: American Association for Higher Education.

Spitzberg, B. H. (1995). The conversational skills rating scale: An instructional assessment of interpersonal competence. Annandale, VA: Speech [National] Communication Association.

Spitzberg, B. H., & Cupach, W. R. (1984). *Interpersonal communication competence.* Beverly Hills, CA: Sage.

Stevens, D., & Levi, A. (2005). *Introduction to rubrics.* Sterling, VA: Stylus.

Stewart, J. (Ed.). (2002). *Bridges not walls: A book about interpersonal communication* (8th ed.). New York, NY: McGraw-Hill.

Suler, J. (2004). The online disinhibition effect. *Cyber Psychology & Behavior, 7*(3), 321–326.

Suskie, L. (2004). *Assessing student learning: A common sense guide.* Bolton, MA: Anker.

Syre, T. R., & Pesa, J. A. (2001). Teaching portfolios: Suggested contents. *College Student Journal, 35,* 260-261.

Tannen, D. (1998). *The argument culture.* New York, NY: Random House.

Taylor, J. (2000). On being an exemplary lesbian: My life as a role model. *Text & Performance Quarterly, 20,* 58-73.

Teven, J. J. (2001). The relationships among teacher characteristics and perceived caring. *Communication Education, 50,* 159-169.

Teven, J. J., & McCroskey, J. C. (1997). The relationship of perceived teacher caring with student learning and teacher evaluation. *Communication Education, 46,* 1-9.

Thweatt, K. S., & McCroskey, J. C. (1998). The impact of teacher immediacy and misbehaviors on teacher credibility. *Communication Education, 47,* 348-358.

Trenholm, S., & Jensen, A. (2004). *Interpersonal communication* (5th ed.). New York, NY: Oxford University Press.

Turner, P. K. (2001). Central States outstanding teaching award winners: Wisdom, eloquence, and a little bit of yourself: A philosophy for teaching. *Communication Studies, 52,* 272-277.

Vangelisti, A. L. (1999). Evaluating the process. In A. L. Vangelisti, J. A. Daly, & G. W. Friedrich (Eds.), *Teaching communication: Theory, research, and methods* (2nd ed., pp. 409-423). Mahwah, NJ: Erlbaum.

Verderber, K. S., & Verderber, R. F. (2004). *Inter-Act: Interpersonal communication concepts, skills, and contexts* (10th ed.). New York, NY: Oxford University Press.

Verderber, K. S., Verderber, F. V., & Berryman-Fink, C. (2006). *Inter-Act: Using interpersonal communication skills* (11th ed.). New York, NY: Oxford University Press.

Wachowski, A., & Wachowski, L. (Producers/Directors). (1999). *The matrix* [Motion picture]. United States: Warner Brothers.

Walther, J. B. (1992). Interpersonal effects in computer-mediated interaction: A relational perspective. *Communication Research, 19*(1), 52-91.

Walther, J. B. (1996). Computer-mediated communication: Impersonal, interpersonal, and hyperpersonal interaction. *Communication Research, 23*(1), 3-44.

Wambach, C., & Brothen, T. (1997). Teacher self-disclosure and student classroom participation revisited. *Teaching of Psychology, 24,* 262-263.

Wanzer, M. B., & Frymier, A. B. (1999). The relationship between student perceptions of instructor humor and students' reports of learning. *Communication Education, 48,* 48-62.

Wanzer, M., Frymier, A., Wojtaszczyk, A. & Smith, T. (2006). Appropriate and inappropriate uses of humor by teachers. *Communication Education, 55,* 178-196.

Wardrope, W. J. (1999). A curricular profile of U.S. communication departments. *Communication Education, 48,* 256-258.

Watzlawick, P., Bavelas, J. B., & Jackson, D. D. (1967). *Pragmatics of human communication: A study of interactional patterns, pathologies, and paradoxes.* New York, NY: Norton.

Wiemann, J. M. (1977). Explication and test of a model of communicative competence. *Human Communication Research, 3,* 195-213.

Wood, J. T. (2007). *Interpersonal communication for everyday encounters* (5th ed.). Belmont, CA: Wadsworth.

Wood, J. T., & Lenze, L. F. (1991). Gender and the development of self: Inclusive pedagogy in interpersonal communication. *Women's Studies in Communication, 14,* 1-23.

Worley, D. W. (2001). Central States outstanding teaching award winner: A teaching philosophy. *Communication Studies, 52,* 278-283.